Halley &HIS COMET

To my wife, with all my love

Halley

&HIS COMET

PETER LANCASTER-BROWN

BLANDFORD PRESS
POOLE · NEW YORK · SYDNEY

First published in the UK 1985 by
Blandford Press, Link House, West Street,
Poole, Dorset BH15 1LL.

Copyright © 1985 Peter Lancaster-Brown

Reprinted 1985 (twice)

Distributed in the United States by
Sterling Publishing Co., Inc.,
2 Park Avenue, New York, N.Y. 10016

British Library Cataloguing in Publication Data

Lancaster Brown, Peter
  Halley and his comet.
  1. Halley's comet
  I. Title
  523.6′4   QB723.H2

ISBN 0 7137 1447 6

Typeset by Megaron Typesetting,
Bournemouth, England

Printed in Great Britain by
Mackays, Chatham

Contents

THE ASTRONOMER'S LOVE SONG

No more I feel the potent spell
  of Jupiter or Mars
Or know the magic peace that fell
  Upon me from the Stars

A fiercer flame – comet-lore –
  Consumes my spirit now;
I cry to you still heavens above,
  'Oh! Halley's, where art
thou?'

Anonymous author *Punch* May 1910

Historians of Science recoil from
the irrationality of their heroes.

Arthur Koestler

Introduction

N 18 MAY 1910 a London correspondent based in Accra, West Africa, wrote home: '. . . Here everyone has gone mad over it, and we all get up at 4 am, and sit and gaze at it till it gets light. It is *the* most wonderful thing ever seen. The comet itself never rises far above the horizon, but its tail, which stands straight up, is like the rays of a very powerful searchlight – so long, that it reaches from the horizon to the very roof of the heavens; and so broad that it occupies roughly one fourth of the arc of the sky; and its light is so powerful that combined with Venus (which is also lovely just now), it has almost the effect of a midnight Sun. The natives are frightened to death of it, and will have it that it means an earthquake is coming . . .'

The comet in question was of course Halley's famous comet when it returned to the Sun in 1910 and people throughout the world stared in wonder or in horror of it.

Edmond Halley (1656-1742) did not discover the comet which bears his name. What he did was to solve the long-standing riddle about the path – or orbit – of a comet he'd seen in 1682 and predict it would return again in 1759 . . .

Halley was a younger contemporary of his friend Isaac Newton (1642-1727). Newton's and Halley's fame is linked in the production of Newton's book *Principia*, perhaps the greatest scientific work ever written. It was Halley who provided the stimulus and motivation for Newton, then

1

a Cambridge recluse, to set down his thoughts on gravitation and write his book; he was Newton's editor, confidant, champion and finally his publisher. Without Halley's encouragement and unstinting help it is doubtful if Newton's work would have seen the light of day. While it was Newton who deciphered the riddle of cometary motions and found they obeyed the same laws as the planets, it was Halley who took Newton's researches a step further and brought them to a practical solution.

Newton's life is reasonably well documented from the time of his birth. We know a good deal about his eccentricities, his innermost thoughts, his religious mania, his preferences in food and even the colour of his domestic furnishings. Because of his life-long habit of submitting all his private letters and scientific papers to repeated drafts and never willingly disposing of a single piece of paper on which he had committed his thoughts, they mostly survive and now provide original sources to flesh out his life. Ironically, in contrast, Halley, possessed with an outgoing nature, comes down to us as a much more shadowy figure. Most of his private papers and letters are lost, and consequently his biography is a patchy one; information about him has to be gleaned from the diaries and letters of contemporaries who were sometimes jealous of his accomplishment or not always in sympathy with him. We know next to nothing about the day-to-day happenings of his boyhood in the City of London where he lived through the Plague and the Fire; we know very little of his youth as a scholar at St Paul's School nor his life at Oxford. While his marriage was a long and happy one, we only have occasional glimpses of it. On the more intriguing aspects of his life, including a spell as a special secret envoy for Queen Anne and the rumours that dogged him, we can only speculate. In his own time Halley's scientific reputation was overwhelmed by Newton's unique genius, and because of his disesteem among churchmen as an alleged heretic, his stature as a powerful, original thinker was not generally appreciated by his peers. Only generations later was his particular brand of genius recognized. Nowadays he is acclaimed as a scientist of the first magnitude. In his lifetime his personal qualities endeared him to princes and servants alike. He was never prejudiced nor jealous of others' achievements. In contrast to his taciturn, dour friend Newton, who seldom smiled, he was possessed of good humour, was candid and fearless in his judgement yet always generous in his dealings with his fellow men. If Halley had one obvious fault, it was of too much forbearance of Newton who in later years sometimes behaved like a despot. As men of sharply contrasting temperaments, their long friendship was indeed a strange one. There were periods of coolness and disagreements and towards the end hints of open hostility with suggestions that Halley's invective hastened Newton's death. Nevertheless, the fruit of their early friendship produced *Principia*; their association was a unique amalgam of genius and remarkable talent that provided a stepping-stone to scientific fame for both.

*   *   *

When man first began to observe the heavens, he puzzled over the appearance of comets which are unlike other celestial objects. The word itself is derived from the Greek *kometes* meaning literally: 'the hairy one', but it was probably the Egyptians who first coined the description 'a hairy star' when alluding to comets and then sometimes represented them by an ideographic hieroglyph similar to the one they used for their sky-goddess Nut, complete with long female tresses as representative of their streaming tails. In another guise the Egyptians also likened some of them (the Sungrazers) to the Bennu or Phoenix – the legendary bird which was consumed by fire and then rose from the ashes. In contrast to the Egyptians, the ancient Chinese likened comets more to brooms or besoms – hence the transient broom or besom stars recorded in their chronicles.

In the early seventeenth century, Kepler believed comets were as numerous as the fishes in the sea, and present-day researches confirm his ideas. They are certainly the most numerous class of body in the solar system and probably swarm in vast numbers round other stars.

Unlike Halley's comet and other bright comets, most of those discovered today remain invisible to the naked eye and require long exposures with large photographic telescopes to render them visible.

In spite of the great advances made in modern astronomical researches, comets remain among the most enigmatic of the nearer celestial bodies. While Newton and Halley solved the long-standing riddle about their orbits, which had puzzled astronomers since early times, no answer was immediately forthcoming about their physical nature or their origins. Even today the nature and origins of comets is highly controversial. A typical comet is usually seen to consist of four parts: the cloud-like head, called the *coma*; the star-like centre, called the *nucleus*; the tail (or tails); and a surrounding cloud of highly tenuous hydrogen gas only detectable in instruments located outside the Earth's atmosphere (*Fig. 1*). Sometimes, to confuse matters, no nucleus is seen, and in fainter telescopic comets there is little or no visible tail.

Comets are certainly gaseous bodies and related to 'shooting' stars,

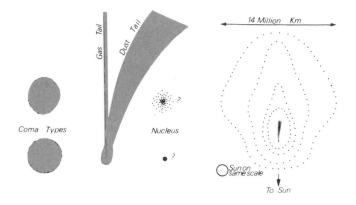

Fig. 1   The principal structural parts of a comet: figure (right) indicates the limits of the hydrogen gas envelope of comet Bennett 1970 II as scanned from the Orbiting Geophysical Observatory-5 in Lyman-alpha light. The different contour boundaries represent different densities of tenuous hydrogen gas surrounding the normally visible parts of the comet (shown in the centre).

these days more correctly called meteors or meteoroids. A simplistic picture of a comet may be likened to a cloud of meteors surrounded, or embedded, in a nebulous envelope of tenuous gasses made up of various constituents all travelling in orbit around the Sun in a closed path usually in the shape of a distended ellipse. The most enigmatic part of a comet is the nucleus, or core. While some astronomers even doubt its reality, consensus opinion generally supports the idea that a slow-spinning agglomeration of matter exists as a small discrete body at a comet's gravitational centre.

At this stage it may be well to draw attention to the sometime mistaken lay notion concerning the apparent motions of comets. Even in serious literature many authors are guilty of committing a howler in the use of the simile: 'It shot across the sky as swift as a comet.' While many comets may be travelling at speeds of several hundred kilometres per second, this is not readily apparent to an observer watching from Earth. A meteor will most certainly appear to shoot swiftly across the heavens in a flash but not so a comet. Unlike a shooting star, which in reality is a tiny fragment broken off a comet, caught and then burnt up in our atmosphere, a comet is situated far beyond this distance, and its movements to the naked eye

4

against the backcloth of stars will only be apparent from night to night observations.

At each approach to the Sun during its known two-thousand-year history, Halley's comet has always been a spectacular object in the night skies. It makes its round trip in a period that varies between seventy-four and seventy-nine years, and in the past its regular apparitions have coincided with some notable historical events. At its closest rendezvous with the Sun it passes inside the orbit of Venus; at its farthest it travels out beyond the orbit of Neptune. In 1910 its tail reached a length of more than 160 million kilometres – a distance greater than that from the Earth to the Sun.

At its 1910 apparition the Earth actually passed through the tail of Halley's comet. Newspapers, before the event, played up the predicted close encounter in dramatic fashion, and as a result many became frightened about the possibility of a global catastrophe. A man in Spain jumped to his death, while in the United States itinerant patent medicine vendors conned the gullible into buying comet pills to ward off the anticipated dire effects. On 19-20 May 1910 the time of the 'collision' came and went but apparently with no readily observable effects. It is known that the Earth has passed through the tail of Halley's comet several times before in history, and nowadays some believe these periodic encounters may be very significant in the destiny of our planet . . .

In earlier times the sudden appearances of brilliant comets played an important role in astrological prognostications: they were cited as portenders or war, plague, famine and the deaths of notables. Some astrologers went so far as to claim that comets actually carried pestilence in their resplendent tails. However, following a better understanding of comets, these former superstitions were gradually laughed out of court by more enlightened thinkers. It was a surprise when in the late 1970s two of the world's leading scientists resurrected the old ideas. They claimed that when the Earth passes through the tails of comets, cosmically spawned bacteria are introduced into the atmosphere and Halley's comet itself may be directly responsible for periodic outbreaks of disease at intervals of seventy-four to seventy-nine years, coinciding with its varying orbital periods.

While these claims are hotly contested by others, it is clear that from evidence provided by meteorites, 'organized' elements similar to those found on Earth exist elsewhere in space and life may have seeded the earth from cosmic regions.

Until the late 1950s the study of comets was a somewhat neglected backwater of astronomy left in the hands of a few specialists. Astronomers for the most part were preoccupied with the study of remote stars and galaxies. The advent of the Sputnik and the space age which followed changed all that. Comets are now in the forefront of modern research, for it is recognized that they may provide the key to the yet unsolved question of how the solar system evolved in its 4.5-billion-year history. Halley's comet, in particular, provides a unique opportunity for the study of a comet at close quarters by space probes and the whole new range of sophisticated instruments now used by astronomers.

1 · Comets in History

*Comets importing change of times and states
Brandish your crystal tresses to the sky,
And with them scourge the bad revolting stars
That have consented unto Henry's death.*

HENRY VI PART I, ACT 1, SCENE 1.

HEN SHAKESPEARE wrote these lines around 1592, he was reflecting some ambivalent and lingering age-old beliefs fostered by earlier astrologers about the profound influence of comets in affecting the destiny of mankind.

Dictionaries of the age confirm that *comet* was often cited as a synonym for presage, and in everyday language, as well as poetic, people used the word comet to mean punish or to scourge. The Bard himself makes several other allusions to comets. In Hamlet, for example, he writes: 'As Stars with trains of fire dews of blood/Disasters in the Sun.'

While in the latter passage the name comet is not spelled out, it nevertheless is implied in the guise of an 'evil star', viz, *disaster*, from the Latin *dis*, with evil sense, and *astrum*, a star, destiny. Nowadays it is no coincidence the word most widely used to express calamity and misfortune has its origin in the older allusion to comets.

According to Greek and Roman writers, the role of comets as portents and influences in the affairs of men had its origins in Babylonia, and these ideas were later passed on to their Egyptian contemporaries; in turn the Greeks and the Romans included comets in their astrologies. While there were stargazers long before the Babylonians and the Egyptians, we have no evidence what they believed about comets. The astronomer-priests of the pre-literate European Megalith Age, circa 4000-1500 BC, left artefactual remains like Stonehenge from which it is possible to surmise

7

how they followed the movements of the Sun and Moon, but they tell us absolutely nothing about the shifts of comets. Although several Greek and Roman writers relate how the Babylonians and the Egyptians before them were very interested in comets, we can find no unambiguous references to them in surviving earlier sources.

A Babylonian comet frequently cited in popular literature is one supposed to have been seen in 1140 BC. However, this interpretation relies on a nineteenth-century translation of a cuneiform text which is faulty, and – in truth – all manner of heavenly events may be interpreted from it depending on the particular bias of the scholar. Discounting the vague speculations made about possible references to comets contained in ancient Middle Eastern cosmic legends, it is not before the seventh century BC one can find a reliable, *sure* reference to a comet anywhere in the world and this is from a Chinese source!

This lacuna in exact knowledge about comets before early Greek and Roman times is a strange one, for the Babylonians and the Egyptians were undoubtedly skilled observers. Their surviving astronomical texts spell out the names of the Sun, Moon, the brighter stars and all the planets then known, but nowhere do we find even the common name which the Babylonians or the Egyptians used when referring to comets. While we have it on the authority of Greek writers that the Egyptians alluded to comets as 'hairy stars', in no Egyptian text yet deciphered is even this claim actually confirmed. Apart from a few enigmatic depictions of a figure like the Egyptian sky-goddess Nut, where she is shown wearing long tresses as a 'hairy' celestial sign, and some equally tantalizing depictions of the Phoenix in the form of the sacred Bennu bird as 'the flying star', the local record for *possible* comets is as barren as that of their Mesopotamian neighbours.

When Seneca, tutor to Nero, decided to take up the study of comets almost two thousand years ago, he too was puzzled by lack of original sources predating the Roman and Greek civilizations. He noted that Conan, a third-century BC astronomer who had made contact with the Egyptians and gleaned from them many ancient observations including a catalogue of eclipses, did not mention comets once. The earliest second-hand reference he found was in Herodotus, who related that in the fifth century BC an Egyptian prophet by name of Sonchês had passed on his knowledge about comets to Pythagoras, and this was the source that claimed comets were astronomical bodies similar to the wandering stars (the planets). Since that time, however, Aristotle had refuted the idea and placed comets as objects occurring in the Earths's atmosphere, and they were therefore a meteorological phenomenon, not celestial. Those who had agreed with Pythagoras were Apollonius of Myndus, Anaxagoras, Hippocrates of Chios and several others. Nevertheless, by Seneca's time the opinion of Aristotle carried so much weight it had become the dogma of the Roman world.

Seneca, ignoring Aristotle's opinion, revived the older ideas and saw comets as true celestial bodies. One of the best second-hand sources he studied was left by Diodorus Siculus, writing about 44 BC. He claimed that the Chaldeans (the Babylonians) and the Egyptians not only considered comets of importance in predicting mundane events on Earth but that the Chaldeans were able to predict their heavenly movements as they were able to predict (lunar) eclipses. On the face of it, this claim – if it were true – is a startling one, for it was not until the joint efforts of Newton and Halley in the latter part of the seventeenth century that the movements of comets were understood in the modern era. However, what Diodorus claimed for the Babylonians was hearsay, and he in turn was only borrowing from older Greek writers whose works were lost even by Seneca's time. Alexandre Pingré (1711-96), one of the greatest investigators of ancient comets, checked back to the original Greek text and discovered earlier astronomers had read too much into the vague claims made by Diodorus.[1] A similar type of myth, perpetuated into the twentieth century, claimed the Babylonians were able to predict eclipses of the Sun, and this is now known to be totally unfounded.

In *Quaestiones naturales*, Seneca summed up his own ideas about comets for posterity. He reemphasized his belief that comets were true astronomic bodies and moved in paths like those of the planets; only in physical appearance did they differ from the other celestial wanderers. However, he was relying on his instincts as a natural philosopher just as Aristotle had done four centuries before him when the Greek had demoted comets from the celestial sphere to the meteorological regions. Seneca had no sure proofs; these were beyond his own means, but he knew that in the future knowledge would advance. This led him to predict with confidence that 'some day a man will arise who will prove beyond doubt the true paths and nature of comets . . .'

Little did Seneca realize the road to truth would be such a long one: that for one man the task was too much and it would take sixteen hundred years after his own forced suicide in AD 65 – a victim of Nero's revenge – to get at even half the truth and almost two thousand years to reach the verge of the whole truth . . .

After the death of Seneca, the study of comets in the Western World made no advance; in actuality, it regressed, for the Church in early Christendom overwhelmingly favoured the Aristotelian view of comets. This combined with the Church's adoption of the Ptolemaic system, which had the Earth at the centre and focus of the planetary system, crippled free thinking until the Renaissance. Not until Nicolaus Copernicus published his monumental book *De Revolutionibus Orbium Coelestium* (*On the Revolutions of the Heavenly Spheres*) in 1543 were the constraints imposed by the old dogma cast off.

Even this was a hard struggle for people whose ideas were steeped in medievalism. The Danish astronomer Tycho Brahe (1546-1601), who contributed important basic observations to the understanding of the new astronomy, could never accept Copernicanism in its entirety and died believing Ptolemy's geocentric system with an all-dominant Earth was fundamentally the more correct one in spite of its many drawbacks.

Before Tycho Brahe, few observers in the West made much of comets; they were the province of the astrologers, and since Aristotle's weighty authority dominated, the 'science' of comets was to be studied as part of *physica* – or those phenomena relating to the Earth's atmosphere, not beyond it. Apart from the dreary old prognostications about the fate of popes and kings and the spread of pestilence, comets were in limbo. Not until 1238 is there a glimmer of true cometary science when the author of an anonymous treatise noticed (correctly) that *bright* comets rarely appear except near the Sun. The next glimmer we owe to Regiomontanus (Peter Müller 1436-76), who suggested that the true distance of comets could be gauged by the application of simple trigonometry and then noting any displacement, or parallax, against the stars. Unfortunately the results he and his helpers derived from this method were erroneous, but they were on the right track. So, too, was the physician Dr Jerome Cardano (1501-76), primarily an astrologer and author of over one hundred books, who suggested that comets lay beyond the Moon and not in the upper atmosphere as generally supposed. Cardano, however, offered no evidence to support his idea; this was left to Tycho who with the help of observer friends in Nuremberg and Prague showed by the parallax method, first suggested by Regiomontanus, that the bright comet of 1577 lay beyond the Moon and probably revolved in a circular orbit.

Earlier in Europe, in 1531, Petrus Apianus (Peter Apian) noted (correctly) that comet tails always appeared to be directed away from the Sun (*Fig. 2*). However, this phenomenon was known to Chinese astronomers as far back as AD 800, and it was probably unwritten knowledge dating back to much earlier times. It was broadly hinted at by

Seneca when he noted the 'rays' of comets always pointed away from the Sun.

While Shakespeare, in Merry England, was busy penning his age-old lines about the dire influences of comets on the fate of mankind, across in Prague, Johannes Kepler (1571-1630), another genius but of a different bent, was busy at work providing the lynch-pin to ideas that one day would tie comets and planets in a common bond and lead to a clearer understanding of how celestial objects moved in their tracks. Kepler became interested in comets when as a small child his mother roused him from his bed to witness the spectacular comet of 1577 – the very comet observed by Tycho and his friends which helped sweep aside the Aristotelian dogma and restore comets to their true realm among the planets. This comet made a deep impression on the sleepy-eyed young Kepler. It was remarkable this should be the very object to stimulate his interest to take up an astronomical career and later become Tycho's protégé.

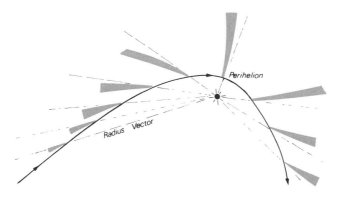

Fig. 2   Comet tails, especially the spectacular dust tails, always point away from the Sun, but they generally lag behind the Comet-Sun line (the radius vector).

In due course it was Tycho's painstaking observations of the planets – especially Mars – made to discredit Copernicanism which, passing into Kepler's hands, ironically provided the indisputable truth of it . . .

Kepler himself became an assiduous observer of all the bright comets in his time. On 23 September 1607 he first saw from the vantage point of one of Prague's picturesque bridges over the river Moldau what was later to become known as Halley's comet. It was Kepler's observations in 1607 that assisted Halley in his later researches into the comet.

However, it was not Kepler's observations of comets which provided his subsequent fame. In fact, Kepler's mind, like Tycho's, was also steeped in medievalism; in his own lifetime he was never aware he had provided the very means to the true understanding of how comets moved, but this needed the genius of Isaac Newton to exploit later in the century.

What Kepler did discover were three laws about planetary motions. He hit upon these discoveries in the course of reconciling the detailed observations of Mars made by Tycho with the idea of it following a circular path as it orbited the Sun.

Copernicus in restating the heliocentric nature of the solar system, first fostered by the Greeks, also accepted in toto the old Hellenic ideal of circular paths for the planets. Kepler now sought to put Tycho's observations to the test – not to discredit the old notions of circular motion but to see whether they might help him correct existing planetary tables which were notoriously unreliable.

Kepler soon discovered Tycho's observations were no help in resolving the discrepancies. This was a great puzzle to him because he knew Tycho's observations of Mars were the most accurate ever made.

He worked on the problem intermittently for eight years and finally exhausted every combination of circular motion for Mars which the ingenuity of his mind could elaborate. Finally he came face to face with the reality of his failure. Surely the Greeks – or God – could not be wrong? Kepler was a religious man. It was always supposed that the Creator would choose the simplest and most perfect of shapes for his creations to revolve in their orbits round the Sun. For two thousand years – since Pythagoras and Aristotle – the idea of the perfect circle had been a dominant part of man's philosophy, and Christianity had adopted it willingly. But the early Christian Church had also adopted the now proven false Ptolemaic system. Could the Church be wrong again? The Greek geometer Apollonius of Perga had described other curves which could be derived from sectioning a cone – the ellipse, the parabola and the hyperbola (*Fig. 3*). However, the Greeks and those who followed them had hitherto regarded these curves simply as objects of amusing speculation with no practical applications in nature.

Intuitively Kepler was drawn to consider the ellipse, for he had already thought about a slightly oval orbit for Mars and the idea that the Sun might be displaced as a point of revolution. In many ways an ellipse was much like a circle whereas the parabola and hyperbola were open-ended

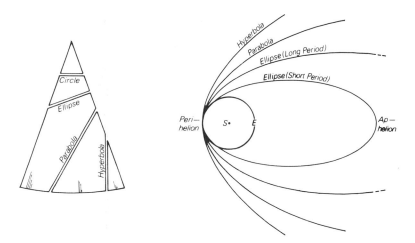

Fig. 3   Conic sections and cometary orbits: (left) A cone may be sectioned to produce a circle, an ellipse, a parabola and a hyperbola. (Right) Near perihelion it is often hard to distinguish between the different cometary orbits.

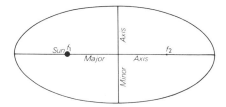

Fig. 4   The properties of an ellipse. The eccentricity is measured by expressing the distance between the two foci, f_1 (Sun) and f_2, in terms of the length of the major axis.

curves. The circle and ellipse only differed in the fact that the circle has one focus while the ellipse has two (*Fig. 4*). In using the circle to fit Tycho's observations, Kepler had placed the Sun at the exact centre and then experimented by offsetting it; now in trying the ellipse he first placed it exactly at the centre of the largest diameter *between* the two foci. As he traced out the path of Mars, it seemed to fit the new curve, and he was buoyant with hope, but continuing the process, the path of Mars slowly began to diverge and finally it broke away from the elliptic track

13

altogether. Yet Kepler was not too downhearted; he had suspected this might happen by positioning the Sun *between* the two foci. He still had a trick up his sleeve. The two foci were all important – or at least *one* might be . . .

He shifted the position of the Sun to fit exactly over one of the two foci. Then he painstakingly retraced the motion of the planet again to fit the curve. Soon his pulse began to beat faster for he had completed a quarter of the motion without deviation; half the motion was then accounted for and still no deviation. Victory was his. He knew now the second half of the ellipse would fit exactly like the first half.

Kepler had made the most important discovery ever about the movement of one celestial body round another. The reason for the existing planetary tables being in error was clear. The Greeks had been deceived; even Copernicus was deceived, then he himself until . . . All the time the evidence had been there but not recognized because until Tycho made his exacting observations of Mars none were accurate enough to throw doubt on the classic theory.

He checked his elliptic theory against the movements of the other planets and the Moon; in turn they all confirmed they moved in a similar fashion to Mars, thus vindicating the idea of the universality of nature's laws. Now he could write down his discovery as a definite law: *Planets revolve in elliptic orbits about the Sun, which occupies the common focus of all these orbits.*

It had struck him earlier that if the planets and the Moon were moving in oval paths, their speed, or velocity, was not constant but depended on what part of the curve of the oval they were moving in. The same would hold true for his newly discovered elliptical orbits. This insight, actually discovered before the first law, provided him with a second universal law: *If a line is drawn from the centre of the Sun to any planet, this line as it is carried forward by the planet sweeps out over equal areas in equal portions of time* (*Fig. 5*).

In discovering both his laws Kepler's draft calculations made over the long years covered nine hundred folio pages in small handwriting. He published his two laws in 1609 when he was thirty-eight years old in his book *Astronomia nova aitiologetos* (*New Astronomy*). The book, although difficult reading, was widely circulated. One copy was read by Kepler's English correspondent, the mathematician Thomas Harriot. It was also read by Harriot's friend, an obscure knight by name of Sir William Lower who had estates near Ilfracombe in Devonshire.

Lower and Harriot made accurate observations of Halley's comet in 1607, but these useful observations were lost for nearly two centuries and remained unknown in Halley's and Newton's time. The most remarkable thing, however, was Lower's insight about the movements of comets. After reading Kepler's *New Astronomy*, he commented on it in a letter to Harriot, dated 1610, noting almost innocently: '. . . for me thinks it shews a way to the solving of the unknowne *walks of comets.*'

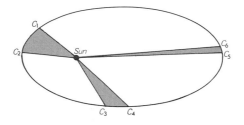

Fig. 5   Kepler's second law (of equal areas). A comet (or any other body in elliptical orbit) takes the same time in moving from $C_1 - C_2$ and $C_3 - C_4$, $C_5 - C_6$. The swept area $C_1 - S - C_2 = C_3 - S - C_4 = C_5 - S - C_6$.

Kepler's *New Astronomy* did exactly that – except no one else, not even its author, realized it. Kepler himself believed the comets were exceptions to universal laws and they pursued straight, rectilinear, paths whereas Tycho Brahe believed them to have a circular motion. We do not know how Harriot reacted to Lower's suggestion or whether he even gave it a second thought, but it is remarkable that what Kepler had overlooked and what everybody else had overlooked as a consequence of the new *universal* elliptical planetary laws was clearly seen by this obscure Englishman with no pretensions to high science. Because this correspondence lay forgotten in a private archive until rescued by a German visitor to England in 1784, Lower's name plays no part in the scientific detective game which involved some of the greatest intellects of the seventeenth century in attempts to unlock the secrets of cometary movements.

In 1619 two great comets were seen, the second of which was of unusual brilliance and remained visible over the period November 1618 until January 1619. Kepler and his contemporaries were keenly interested in these comets, and subsequently a plethora of discourses, pamphlets and books were inspired by this unprecedented celestial threat. The debate concerning their true nature sparked off a great controversy between Horatio Grassi (a Jesuit priest), Galileo, Mario Guiducci (a pupil of Galileo), and Kepler.

On the issue of comets we find Galileo anything but the enlightened scholar that tradition has him. He adopted the backward-looking Aristotelian view about the nature of comets to try to discredit Tycho's claim that the comet of 1577 lay beyond the Moon. Galileo's contributions to cometary science is a very indirect one and relates to his earlier experiments with falling weights in which he foreshadowed two of the great laws about universal gravitation later formulated by Isaac Newton.

Even Kepler's views on comets was a mixture of medieval and avant-garde. A sometime astrologer himself, to make ends meet – one story relates he chose his second wife by consulting horoscopes – he restricted the role of comets to portents for kings only while the advent of new stars (novae) were portents for states, viz, the appearance of a new star meant the emergence of a new republic.

In his book *De cometis*, published in 1619, Kepler restated his old views that the paths of comets were always rectilinear (straight). He believed they were steered in their courses by astrologically minded daemons under the will of God, who sent them as a sign as he might do with 'a seamonster washed ashore'. Physically, he believed, comets were condensations in the all-pervading ether, a kind of celestial 'abscess' of impurities, partly transparent but capable of dimming the light of the Sun on important occasions. Space was full of comets as the sea was full of fishes. A comet was not a self-luminous body; he even came close to modern ideas when he claimed the deflection of the tail might be attributed to refraction suffered by the Sun's rays in passing through the head of a comet – or the matter ejected from the comet being brought to rest. And like the medieval astronomers and the Greeks before them, he claimed the Earth's contact with a comet's tail could render the atmosphere impure and thereby cause widespread mortality.

Since 1609, when Kepler published his two laws about elliptical planetary motions, his mind had never left the problem. In spite of his great discovery, he knew, almost intuitively, that this work was only partially complete.

The kind of solar system he believed in was not just a mere assemblage of isolated planets revolving about the Sun at their common focus. It was a group of closely associated bodies. While he had solved the problem of how each of them moved individually, still hidden from him was the greatest truth – the unifying principle or law which explained the common family bond between them all.

His search for this missing law he likened to probing inside God's mind to extract the scheme he had decided upon when he created the system of the planets. For Kepler it was a search extending over many years and one of frustration and despair. It was a pioneer archetypal numbers' game of a kind pursued by generations of astronomers who followed him. After he had pondered the line of attack, he decided the common bondage of the planets was something to do with the time of their periodic revolutions round the Sun in relation to their distances out from the Sun. Perhaps it was a very simple law? Mercury, the innermost planet, revolved round the Sun fastest of all in fifty-eight days while Saturn, the outermost planet, was the slowest, taking over twenty-nine years. There had to be some connecting theme. First, in the hope it was a straightforward relationship, he tried simple arithmetical relationships between the revolutionary periods of the planets at their distances out. He exhausted every numerical combination but had no success. Undaunted he pressed on. God, perhaps in his wisdom, had been more subtle; now Kepler tried the squares of the periods and distances. Again failure greeted him. Still undaunted, he tried using the cubes of the periods and distances, but not a glimmer of any grand law revealed itself.

Setting aside the problem for some time, he then returned fresh to the attack. He decided to try combinations involving the simple periods and the squares of the distances. For the first time there was a hint of approximation; nothing to allow him to establish a law but enough to encourage him to pursue this line . . .

He now tried simple multiples of the planets' revolution periods and the squares of their distances. However, no matter how he arranged the numbers, it was all in vain. He abandoned the simple periods and distances and substituted the relationship between the squares of these quantities. Still gaining absolutely no encouragement from this, he rose even higher to consider the cubes of the periods and distances – yet with the same negative results.

Finally, in a last-ditch attempt to solve the riddle, he decided to mix squares and cubes. He chose the proportions existing between the squares of the periods and the cubes of the distances . . . He was on the brink of his long-sought-after linking theme for the planets, but now in his feverish haste he committed an arithmetical blunder and the relationship remained hidden. Heartsick at the negative results with this and other combinations he tried, he turned away in despair.

Several months later his instinct drew him back to reconsider the problem. In the interim his mind had subconsciously dwelt on the various arrangements and combinations. Why hadn't they worked? In particular

17

the proportion existing between the squares of the periods and the cubes of the distances was the one that kept returning time and time again. Now, as if guided by some friendly spirit, he girded himself for one final attempt. Perhaps there was something he had overlooked. Almost at once he detected a careless error in his old computations. On the desk top before him it was almost there . . . The square of Jupiter's period is to the square of Saturn's period as to the cube of Jupiter's distance is to same fourth term . . . Please God, let this fourth term be the cube of Saturn's distance . . .

With a trembling hand he reploughed through his calculations, his brain fevered in expectation. Again in haste he botched some simple addition but soon realized this so he backtracked once more . . . The result was the cube of Saturn's distance!

However, after the long pursuit for the missing relationship it made him suspicious of victory. Now he feared some demon mocked him. He repeated the work, checking every stage of it. Then he tried the proportion, the square of Jupiter's period to the square of Mars's period as the cube of Jupiter's distance to a fourth term . . . which, in due course, he found to his utter relief to be the cube of the distance of Mars. The struggle was over. Now he could write down his third law: *The squares of the periods in which the planets describe their orbits are proportional to the cubes of their mean distances from the Sun.*

In 1619 he published it in his new book *Harmonices mundi* (*Harmony of the Universe*) where he restated his beliefs in the dynamical harmony of the solar system. He wrote: 'God is vindicated and now I indulge my sacred fury! The book is written, to be read either now, or by posterity, I care not which. It may well wait a century for a reader, since God waited six thousand years for an observer!'

Kepler didn't realize his new law brought him to the verge of discovering universal gravitation. But this escaped him. His third law which had taken such an effort to wrest from nature was to be the very stepping-stone from which Newton and others advanced later in the century to find how God's laws actually kept the planets in motion and how even the long-errant comets obeyed them.

Note

[1] Diodorus mentions several great comets that had appeared in the past. In 371 BC a 'prodigious' comet had shown itself which is reported to have broken up in two parts. Seneca, basing his judgement on comets he had seen in his own time, surprisingly disputed that such a thing could occur. Another comet mentioned

by Diodorus was one in 344 BC which appeared on the occasion when Timolus of Corinth made an expedition to Sicily. One seen in 156 BC after the death of Demetrius, King of Syria, was described: 'as large as the Sun', of a 'red appearance' and 'very fiery'. It was so brilliant, claimed those who saw it, it 'turned night into day' and this must have been one of the brightest ever seen.

The brightest and biggest comet on record appeared sometime in the reign of Mithridates (132-63 BC). This magnificent object was also described by contemporaries as brighter than the Sun. It was watched for seventy nights and became so luminous its radiance blotted out a quarter of the visible stars, and observers reported it was as if the whole heavens were ablaze. No comet seen since has appeared so bright. Although the exact year of its appearance is uncertain, it was undoubtedly a real comet and it is portrayed on a copper coin of the period. On the evidence provided by ancient authors, it is likely the comet of Mithridates was a Sungrazer. The period of this comet is unknown, but one day its orbit may return it to the Sun; if and when this happens, it will provide onlookers with the unique opportunity to view the most spectacular body ever to visit our night skies.

2 · Halley and Newton

N AUGUST 1684, fifty-four years after Kepler's death, a tallish, fair-haired Londoner, troubled by a perplexing mathematical problem to which he could find no solution, rode to Cambridge to consult an older acquaintance.

The traveller was Edmond Halley, then twenty-eight years old; the man he visited was Isaac Newton, fourteen years his senior. Halley's mission – the result of a wager made by Sir Christopher Wren – concerned some consequences following on from Kepler's laws. Newton had been a don at Cambridge since 1667 and had already earned himself a formidable reputation as a brilliant mathematician and experimental philosopher. Halley was a rising young astronomer in Royal Society circles. The pair had met only briefly after Newton had initiated some correspondence requesting observations of bright comets Halley had observed in 1680-1 and in 1682. Now, as a consequence of Halley's decision to consult his more experienced acquaintance about a possible solution to the troublesome mathematical problem, the scene was set for the biggest step forward in astronomy since Galileo applied the telescope to the heavens in 1609 . . .

*　　　　　*　　　　　*

Newton had come up to Trinity College in 1661 from Woolsthorpe in Lincolnshire where he had been born on Christmas Day 1642, the same year Galileo died. Newton's father – a yeoman farmer unable to sign his own name – died three months before his son's birth. From an early age young Isaac developed neurotic tendencies which were probably further engendered by his separation from his mother when early in 1646 she married again and went to live in a neighbouring village at the home of her new husband. Isaac remained behind at Woolsthorpe in the care of his maternal grandmother, and not until his step-father died in 1653 did his mother return to the family manor-house.

As a boy Newton showed a mischievous bent as well as a marked precocity. He was also an excellent model-maker, and there is an apt story illustrating this blend of traits. After reading about the supposed sinister influences of comets, he made lanterns of crimped paper, cunningly illuminated them with candles, and flew them from the tails of kites over the countryside to instil the fear of God into local rustics who, as anticipated, knew all about the consequences of heavenly presages.

However, not until the comet of 1664 appeared in the night skies above Trinity College, when Newton had been at Cambridge for three years, had he the opportunity to observe a real comet at first hand. His Cambridge contemporaries related how the brilliant undergraduate neglected all else to study it. The story goes he even forgot mealtimes and his pet cat grew fat from the food left uneaten on his master's study table.

By this time Newton, although still an undergraduate, had slipped into the role of college recluse and now shunned all but necessary human contact. His obsessional phobia to keep the 1664 comet under constant watch came to light through the husband of Newton's niece, John Conduitt, who was privileged to Newton's later-life reminiscences. According to Conduitt: 'He [Newton] sate up so often long in the year 1664 to observe a comet . . . he found himself much disordered and learned from then on to go to bed betimes.'

Nevertheless, in spite of what he told Conduitt, Newton rarely went to bed early. Throughout his adult life it became common knowledge that he never learnt the habit of regular hours – especially on those occasions when a problem had beset him and a solution was demanded to relieve his pressing thoughts on the matter.

The bright comet of 1664 had caused a stir everywhere. It was discovered in Spain on 17 November 1664 and during the following weeks it was seen through the rest of Europe. Its appearance over London was noted by the diarists Samuel Pepys and his good friend John Evelyn. It was also assiduously observed by Robert Hooke, the 29-year-old curator of experiments at the prestigious, newly created Royal Society of London, whose charter had been granted by Charles II just two years previous. It was to be the Royal Society that provided the back-cloth to future events involving Newton, Halley, Hooke, Flamsteed, Christopher Wren, even Pepys and Evelyn as dramatis personae in the story of the creation of Newton's *Principia* and, afterwards, in the naming of the comet after Halley.

In 1664, however, those events were twenty years in the future, and Edmond Halley[1], born on 29 October 1656 at his father's country house at Haggerston on the outskirts of London, was just eight years old. Nevertheless, there is good reason to suppose that, like Newton, Halley too saw the comet. This would probably have been from his father's town house in Winchester Street. Although biographical details of his early life are very sketchy, we have it on Halley's own admission about his very early love of astronomy. We might surmise, without stretching credulity, that it was the appearance of the bright comet of 1664 which sparked off his interest in much the same fashion the brilliant comet of 1577 had sparked off six-year-old Kepler's life-long interests in astronomy. Whatever, young Halley would only be one among the tens of thousands of Londoners – men and women with babes in arms – who were drawn outdoors to watch with rapt attention the comet of 1664 as it moved ominously above the City.

Pepys, then thirty-one years old, was no kind of astronomer or scientific man and was so busy in his post as Clerk to the Navy he missed getting an early view of the comet. Evelyn had seen it in late November and so had most of his other friends. Now, by Christmas, because the comet was the talk of the London coffee-houses, Pepys decided he must see it for himself. However, because there was a bright moon shining, he failed to catch sight of the celestial visitor as he had no idea in which direction to look for it; but the morning after, having been briefed by others, he was more successful and although he did not think it looked very impressive as a spectacle (few comets do in moonlight), he was aware of its ominous potential since for weeks the City's streets had echoed with the daily cries of war, famine or plague forecast by the pedlars of astrological pamphlets.

The comet stirred in Pepys a desire for more knowledge about comets, and he attended Hooke's second lecture on it held at Gresham College in Bishopsgate, where the Royal Society had their rooms and met every Thursday. Hooke told his audience he believed the comet to be the return of the one seen by Kepler in 1618. Pepys decided he too would like to be a member of the Royal Society; however, soon after joining, his membership lapsed, and he did not rejoin until pressed into doing so in 1680 by Evelyn.

In early 1665 war with the Dutch was in the air again, and when hostilities were officially declared on 22 February, the London astrologers quickly claimed part of their predictions about the presence of the comet was now fulfilled, but they promised worse was still to follow.

In 1665 the devil played into their hands when yet another bright comet was sighted from Nuremberg and was soon seen over London. Those who had scoffed at the first comet began to think again. A double presage was known to have a unique significance.

John Gadbury, an Oxford-educated astrologer and friend of John Aubrey, had a particular specialist interest in comet prognostications. He now had a field-day and would soon write a book about these two presages. Comets, he believed, meant a return of the Black Death. There had been plague attacks in 1527, 1593, 1603, 1625 and 1636 and on these occasions, claimed Gadbury, either a comet or an eclipse, or both, had been seen before the onset of the epidemic. It did not escape Pepys, and other Londoners, that in January 1665 there had been an eclipse of the Moon. The appearance of two comets within the space of a few months and then an eclipse between them was unique. When published in 1665, Gadbury's book *De Cometis*, with its illustrations of the comets (erroneously citing three comets) and the caption doomsday verses, borrowed from the poet Du Bartas, its message was clear enough.

In spite of those who scoffed at such astrological nonsense, like the famous physician Dr Nathaniel Hodges who noted dryly: 'The Mischief is much more in the Predictions of the Stargazers than in the Stars themselves,' there were others who were unsure. When the Plague struck the City in 1665 and then the Great Fire in 1666, the believers could point out that all the prognostications had been fulfilled.

Although Londoner Daniel Defoe (born 1659 or 1660) was even younger than Halley when the two comets appeared, he later evoked the impressionable years of his childhood and the profound effect the two comets had on the City dwellers at street level. In his faction narrative *Journal of the Plague Year* (1722) Defoe writes '. . . a blazing star or comet appeared several months before the Plague and then did the year after another, a little before the Fire.' On the 1664 comet he remarks: '. . . it passed directly over London so that it was plain it imported something peculiar to the city alone . . . it was of a faint, dull languid colour, that its motion was very heavy, solemn and slow, and it accordingly foretold a heavy judgement, slow but severe, terrible and frightful, as was the Plague.'

*　　　*　　　*

In the decades before the 1664 and 1665 comets, there had been one seen in 1652 and another in 1661, but neither caused much of a stir. Now with the two bright comets seen in rapid succession, the events attracted several astronomers into print at a more scientific level than the mischievous tone adopted by Gadbury's book.

Following the appearance of the 1652 comet, Seth Ward, a professor at Gresham College and a friend of Wren, put forward the idea of a circular or even an elliptical orbit for it, reviving Tycho Brahe's ideas. However, again no one apparently took this suggestion seriously, and the Keplerian notion of its path being represented by a straight line remained favourite. Even Hooke, now considered Englands's leading expert on cometary matters, preferred rectilinear paths for all comets, but how he could reconcile this with the idea he had fostered at the lecture attended by Pepys when he professed his belief that the 1664 comet was none other than the great comet of 1618 returning, which implied the 1618 comet must have *turned* somewhere in order to come back again, is not at all clear.

A French astronomer, Adrien Auzout, wrote a paper for the Royal Society's *Philosophical Transactions* in which he claimed (correctly) the path of the 1664 comet lay in one plane (like the paths of the planets), but he still endorsed the (incorrect) theory that it moved constantly in a straight line.

In 1668, Hevelius of Danzig, then recognized as the leading observer in the world, published his book *Cometographia* where he vaguely suggested parabolic orbits for comets but did not offer evidence for the idea. For its time Hevelius's book was a handsome achievement and provided good descriptions of many comets seen in the past as well as his own observations of the 1664 and 1665 comets. He also attempted to classify comet tails by their appearance and shape, and although his depictions sometimes have a rather weird look about them, they represented a step forward in a more scientific understanding of comets. Hevelius's book was to have a profound influence on one of his pupils, an obscure Protestant pastor called Georg Samuel Dörfell, who was to arrive at a true theory of cometary orbits several years before Newton quite independently arrived at similar conclusions. It is doubtful that Newton or Halley in their lifetimes ever knew about Dörfell's work.

By far the most ambitious work on comets attempted in the seventeenth century was that by Stanislas Lubieniczki, a Polish astronomer who wrote a three-part, two-volume work *Theatrum Cometicum*, published in Amsterdam in 1668. Lubieniczki's book was the culmination of what is considered to be the first instance of international co-operation in scientific investigation. After the appearance of the 1664 and 1665 comets he believed it was desirable to have an encyclopedia containing accounts of all the comets ever seen. To this end he circulated a request to more than forty leading astronomers in Europe for material he could include to produce a great history on the subject.

Unfortunately, when completed, the scientific content of Lubieniczki's book was unreliable. Many of the 415 comets he cites are fictitious ones, particularly those invented by chroniclers in the Middle Ages who thought it absolutely essential to have a comet presage announcing the death of any king. In this way there is a fictitious comet recorded as having been seen in AD 814 which allegedly heralded the death of Charlemagne.

Little is known about Lubieniczki. He led an obscure life and became subject to persecution by religious enemies. He died in dramatic circumstances in Hamburg after being poisoned, and most of his works remained unpublished and were subsequently destroyed or lost. Interestingly, a second edition copy of Lubieniczki's book, dated 1681, was found in Newton's library. The work is now very scarce and its existence escaped the eagle eyes of Houzeau and Lancaster when they compiled their hopefully all-embracing *Bibliographie Générale de L'Astronomie*, published in 1887. A feature of Lubieniczki's book are the magnificent illustrations consisting of eighty-three superb plates, many of them double-page width, depicting the paths of various comets, including what has later been identified as Halley's at various apparitions.

Newton's observations of the 1664 and 1665 comets remained unpublished. He was still unknown and was not on the list of the nine invited British virtuosi approached by Lubieniczki to contribute material for his ambitious book. While comets were to fascinate Newton all his life, his feverish mind was constantly busy during his Cambridge years with wide-ranging, multifarious problems in mathematics, optics, alchemy and biblical chronology.

In London the members of the Royal Society were vaguely aware of the brilliant but recluse mathematician at Trinity College, Cambridge, but it was not until he presented his newly invented reflecting telescope to the Society that its members sat up and recognized a new British genius in their midst.

Newton's boyhood experience as a model-maker stood him in good stead with the construction of apparatus for his practical experiments. The superficial impression of Newton, gained from some short biographies, is one of a study-bound genius, his head constantly in books; a man sat rooted at his study desk or gazing into space in his orchard in a state of cogitation. This, however, is only one half of the man, for he was a skilled practical experimenter. Then, after his Cambridge days when he reached high office at the London Mint, he amazed his acquaintances as a person possessing great organizational and administrative abilities. The telescopes he constructed in 1668 and those in later years were made by his own hand, and these were the first reflecting-type telescopes that ever worked.

The telescopes Galileo had fashioned by gleaning ideas from the Dutch were of the *refracting* type, viz, they worked by collecting, then focusing, light passing through spectacle-type transparent glass lenses. But concave mirrors, which collected light then *reflected* and focused it, had been known to the Greeks and, according to legend, used as 'burning glasses'. First to adopt the mirror principle for a telescope design was the Scotsman James Gregory. In 1663 he described a type of telescope with two mirrors, a primary and a secondary made of speculum metal; unfortunately Gregory was not skilled enough to produce a reflecting telescope that worked. His principles were correct, and later in the hands of others he was successful in producing what today is called a Gregorian telescope. In the meantime Newton was inventing another kind of reflector – today known as a Newtonian telescope. His first one was only 15cm long, but it was provided with a magnification of forty times and it performed as well as a refractor-type telescope several metres in focal length.

Not content with his first telescope, Newton improved upon the design and then presented it in late 1671 to the Royal Society to which he was elected soon after.

It was from about this time or even a little earlier that Robert Hooke, still Curator of Experiments at the Society and considered as the leading model-maker and expert in any number of subjects, recognized in Newton a formidable potential rival. Hooke was jealous of the unique position he had long held in the Society. He had been there from the start and he was used to attention being focused on his own scientific achievements. It probably unnerved him to realize that Newton's mathematical abilities far outmatched his own. He criticized Newton's paper on the theory of colours and found to his joy that Newton disliked and shrank back from controversy. Hooke decided to play on what he considered was the Achilles' heel of his potential rival. He was likely relieved and satisfied with his efforts when Newton did not enter freely into Royal Society affairs in London. He took it as a sign of weakness on Newton's part. He himself could remain centre-stage. Hooke, however,

27

little realized that he had made himself a bitter and unforgiving enemy. It was a time-bomb whose long fuse he had lit with his own hand. It would explode in his face a decade later.

In the meantime, yet another potential rival to Hooke was growing up in the wings. After attending St Paul's School, where he became school captain, Halley left for Oxford University. He entered Queen's College in the summer of 1673, when he was seventeen, and arrived, according to one account, with 'a curious apparatus of instruments' provided by the indulgence of his merchant father, a wealthy soapboiler.

These instruments were a telescope and a sextant with which he intended to pursue his studies in astronomy. At St Paul's he had left with the reputation of an excellent scholar and a person who would make his

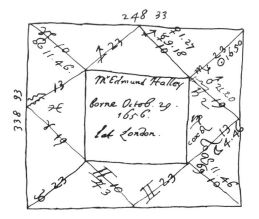

Fig. 6   A facsimile of Halley's horoscope found in the Bodleian Library, Oxford. The astrologer who cast it, likely at the instructions of John Aubrey, is not known with certainty, but it probably was the work of John Gadbury, a contemporary of Halley, who associated comets with the advent of plague. Unlike many of his contemporaries, Halley himself was neither superstitious nor sympathetic to astrology.

mark in the world of science. Already at school he had made his mark as an expert, for according to John Aubrey 'while he was there he was very perfect in caelestiall Globes in so much that I heard Mr Moxton (the Globe-maker) say that if a star were misplaced in the Globe, he would presently find it.'

At Queen's, Halley soon added to his growing reputation, for Aubrey adds: 'at the age of nineteen he solved this useful Probleme in Astronomie never donne before viz. *from 3 distances given from the Sun, and Angles between, to find the Orbe,* for which his name will be ever famous.'

While Aubrey was perhaps overstating Halley's reputation at this time, his work had attracted attention. He was now corresponding regularly with John Flamsteed, appointed by Charles II in 1675 as Astronomer Royal at the newly erected Royal Greenwich Observatory. During university vacations Halley visited Flamsteed and the pair observed together, the Astronomer Royal having taken the very promising Oxford undergraduate ten years his junior under his wing.

Yet Halley grew restless at Oxford and was impatient to make his mark in the world. Before graduating he persuaded his father to support him on an expedition to St Helena in the southern hemisphere to make a catalogue of southern stars. With a star catalogue under his belt he would be an astronomer of some consequence. The southern heavens were much less known than those in the north; except for some constellations formed by the early Dutch voyagers, it was practically virgin territory.

The stars of the northern hemisphere had been mapped out and catalogued many times by astronomers from the time of the Babylonians, but the catalogue made by Tycho Brahe in the immediate pre-telescopic age was still the most accurate and most envied. He had determined places for 777 stars up to the year 1600, and subsequent to this Kepler had extended the master's catalogue to about one thousand stars using observations he had inherited from Tycho.

Hevelius in Danzig was known to be working on yet another catalogue in hopes of gaining more accuracy than that achieved by Tycho, and Flamsteed at Greenwich had also embarked on what was to be a lifetime's work in creating a new, fully comprehensive, star catalogue. But these were long-term programmes of work carried out between other routine observations. By devoting two years of his life to observing stars in the southern hemisphere full time, Halley believed he could produce a catalogue that would bring his name to the forefront of science and earn him the recognition of the leading European astronomers. It was a calculated investment involving two critical years of his life. For the moment, however, Halley was free of financial worries. Although his father's soapboiling business had not been as successful as formerly and he had lost property in the Great Fire, he was still able to support his elder son to the tune of £300 per annum, a very handsome sum in those days. The southern stars, so far much neglected by European astronomers, were a ripe fruit waiting to be picked; if he delayed a year or two until he graduated, someone else might forestall him and reap the harvest.

He was still only twenty years old when he left England in November 1676 as a passenger aboard a British East Indiaman bound for St Helena, a lonely outpost in the South Atlantic. Flamsteed's influence and that of others at the Royal Society had helped him gain the King's ear, and Charles II secured a berth for the young astronomer and a companion by the name of James Clerke (or Clark), whose role in Halley's sojourn in the southern hemisphere remains rather a shadowy one. There is the probability that Clerke was a paid companion, perhaps a chaperon insisted upon by Halley's father only too aware of his son's immaturity.

Halley soon discovered that St Helena was not an ideal locality from which to observe the stars. The small island has a maritime climate and is much affected by cloud and rain. He erected his observatory near Mount Actaeon the island's tallest peak – some two thousand odd feet in height – at a spot overlooking what 145 years later was to be Napoleon Bonaparte's temporary resting-place.

In spite of countless overcast nights, when no stars could be measured, sufficient observations slowly accumulated. With Clerke's help the task was completed. He returned to England in May 1678 with enough basic data to produce his catalogue and draw up a planisphere of the constellations.

Halley also returned to England with gossip dogging his heels concerning his stay in the South Atlantic. From then on there were hints of scandal surrounding his name almost to the end of his life.

If there was substance in the gossip after his immediate return to London, it apparently did him no harm. The catalogue, entitled *Catalogus stellarum australium*, and a planisphere were soon in print. Helped by Flamsteed and others at the Royal Society, including Hooke, who so far had taken kindly to the young astronomer, Halley brought his catalogue and planisphere to the notice of Charles II whose influence had been paramount in securing him passage south.

The King was a dabbler in science himself and had lent his patronage to the Royal Society. No doubt he was highly gratified and flattered to learn that at the hands of Halley he had now gained immortality among the southern stars. Halley had rearranged some southern stars forming part of the old constellation of Argo, known in part to the ancient Greeks, and called the group Robur Carolinum – Charles's Oak. The new constellation was thus dedicated to Charles II and to the oak tree in which the King had taken refuge after the Battle of Worcester in 1651.

As a result of his enterprise, Halley gained Charles's immediate favour.

For his efforts he was awarded his MA degree at Oxford plus the honour of election as a Fellow of the Royal Society. Now, just twenty-two years old, Halley had accomplished what he had set out to do. He had earned himself a reputation and a place among the virtuosi. Flamsteed was impressed enough with the finished catalogue to label Halley, very generously, 'the Southern Tycho'. It was a compliment the Astronomer Royal was to regret in the years ahead.

Halley, rising on the crest of his newly won reputation, was soon on his travels again, this time as the Royal Society's personal representative to Danzig to visit Hevelius.

Hevelius was a corresponding member of the Society and a controversy had arisen over the method he adopted to observe stars for his catalogue. It was now seventy years since Galileo and others had first applied the telescope to look at the night sky, and since then advances had been made by adapting telescopic sights to measuring-instruments to make them more accurate. Hevelius, however, claimed that non-optical open sights, much like those Tycho had used before the telescope, were as good as the new-fangled ones. Flamsteed and Hooke disagreed with this and cast serious doubts on the supposed accuracy of Hevelius's observations. Since the reputation of Hevelius was at stake and the Society had no wish for acrimonious debate, they decided to send Halley, now himself an expert in measuring stars, to study Hevelius's methods and report back. In spite of coffee-house rumours to the contrary, Halley now had a reputation for discretion, and the Council of the Society believed him to be unaffected by prejudice in the matter.

The upshot of the visit was that Halley reported back favourably: he was impressed by the Danzig astronomer's methods. On the face of things Hevelius and Halley had got on famously. However, it subsequently transpired that Halley had not been entirely frank about the state of matters. Later, in a letter to a friend, he privately confessed to having concealed his real opinion of his host's out-dated observing technique for fear of bringing about an early departure to the grave of 'an old peevish Gentleman'.

Flamsteed, in particular, believed Halley had been too generous in his official report about Hevelius. It vexed him because he knew, as everyone else knew, that telescopic sights were a great improvement over the outdated open sights. He probably taxed Halley about his strange attitude in the matter, and this was likely *one* of the triggering causes to the open breach in their friendship that later, on Flamsteed's part, developed into downright hostility. They never made up their differences and the enmity between them lasted almost forty years.

On Halley's part it must be said that Flamsteed was not the easiest man to get on with. Extremely pious, he had taken holy orders and it coloured all his ideas about conduct. In addition Flamsteed had been ill all his life, and this made him tetchy and often short tempered with others. However, there seems to have been more to it than that. Halley, he must soon have recognized, was already his intellectual superior in many respects. He was a much better mathematician and had more insight. In later years rumours had it that Flamsteed had used some of Halley's calculations without acknowledgement about which Halley was annoyed.

It is possible too that shortly after Halley returned from Danzig, Flamsteed overheard some coffee-house gossip about his protégé's alleged amorous exploits. Perhaps these shocked his sense of propriety. Perhaps then he drew conclusions why Halley had been so lenient in his official report about Hevelius's observing methods.

So what were these rumours? Certainly there was nothing committed to print about them for many years. Aubrey in his *Brief Lives* – not published until 1813 – writes obliquely in respect to Halley's sojourn in St Helena and remarks: 'There went over with him (amongst others) a woman, and her husband, who had no child in several yeares; before he came from the Island, she was brought to bed of a Child . . .'

The innuendo is plain, but the truth of it uncertain. Aubrey had a reputation for outrageous statement, even about his friends. Nevertheless, it could be this very episode that Flamsteed is referring to in a bitterly worded letter to Newton some years later when he writes that Halley should 'give us a true account of all his St Helena exploits'.

But another, more serious, charge against Halley was in connection with Hevelius's second wife, Elizabetha.

His first wife had died in 1662, and the following year, now in his fifties, he courted and married a beautiful sixteen-year-old daughter of one of the city's richest merchants. Subsequently he had taught her how to observe, and old prints depict her helping her husband to measure star positions. In 1679, when Halley arrived in Danzig, Elizabetha Hevelius was still a beautiful creature. It must have been a novel experience for the dashing young astronomer from London to be briefed about the use of Hevelius's famous long telescopes, one measuring some 100 metres, by a member of the gentler sex.

Whether Halley actually took advantage of his position while resident in his host's house is not known for certain, but Thomas Hearne, writing years later, makes no uncertain allusion to it. After Halley's portrait was placed by one of Hevelius in the gallery of the Bodleian Library on 13 November 1713, Hearne, in his *Remarks and Collections*, comments: 'And some Persons say that he is very justly placed by Hevelius, because he made him (as they give out) a Cuckold, by lying with his wife, who had a very great Kindness for Mr. Halley, and was (it seems) observed often to be familiar with him.' Yet even Hearne, no friend of Halley and often critical of him (*see below*), after committing the mischief, added: 'But this story I am apt to think is false.'[2]

True story or no, Flamsteed may also have been alluding to this persistent rumour when he wrote to Newton on 7 February 1695: '. . . I have done with him [Halley] who has almost ruined himselfe by his indiscreet behaviour. & you shall hear no more of him from me till wee meet when I shall tell you his history which is too foule and large for a letter.' Unfortunately, this is also a blind alley of innuendo, for we never learn what Flamsteed had to tell Newton. Whatever it was, it doesn't seem to have influenced Newton's own often very strange friendship with Halley, for shortly afterwards he secured him an official position at the Chester Mint.

After his trip to Danzig, little is known about Halley's activities in London during the rest of 1679 and the early months of 1680 except that he immersed himself in the routine business of the Royal Society by day and then by night in astronomical observations. If he had a young man's attachments, or was paying court to any lady, she remains totally anonymous during this period of his life.

It seems, however, he had caught the travel bug and he was soon restless again. Still in receipt of a generous allowance from his father, he conceived a plan to indulge himself in a grand tour of Europe. This would not be the usual routine one of the well-to-do young gentleman – his tour would have a serious scientific purpose. The trip to Danzig were he had spent two months in intellectual pleasures had given him an appetite for European learning and culture. Astronomical research was blossoming on the Continent, and at the Paris Observatory some remarkable new discoveries were being made. He needed a companion and he approached an old school chum, Robert Nelson, son of a rich Turkey merchant and later well known for his religious writings. Nelson was the same age and of similar family background and he had also been elected to the Royal Society shortly after Halley.

Then in November 1680, while Halley and Nelson were still in London, a new bright comet was announced. It wasn't the comet destined to have Halley's name attached to it, that one was still two years off;

however, it was a comet which was to have lasting scientific influence and a few years later bring Halley and Newton together in a close working relationship.

This new comet was discovered by Godfrey Kirch in Coburg, Germany. Although it was just faintly visible to the naked eye, Kirch had actually first spotted it telescopically, and it is the first comet on record to have been discovered this way. By 21 November the comet had rapidly increased in brightness and by the 24th was plainly visible to the unassisted eye. On the 28th it had grown a tail extending to a length of 15°.

Night by night the comet moved towards the twilight sky and closer to the Sun until it became difficult to see. Then it was finally lost from view. Soon after rounding the Sun, at perihelion, it emerged again into the twilight sky, displaying a magnificent tail stretching 70° across the heavens.

It had taken everyone by surprise. It was believed to be a second, new, comet which had become visible after the first one had disappeared in much the same way as two quite independent comets had (genuinely) appeared in succession in late 1664 and early 1665. Flamsteed, however, was one who suspected it was the same comet which had somehow 'about-turned' after approaching the Sun, but his views on how this had been accomplished (by magnetic repulsion) failed to impress others, and, indeed, while Flamsteed was correct in his assumption that the second comet was the returning manifestation of the first one, the rest of his ideas about it were erroneous. Not for some time did most astronomers come round to the idea the two comets were simply one in different modes of its orbit. Newton especially took some convincing and was among the last to accept it.

In London the 'second' comet became the talk of the coffee-houses and taverns. As previously, in 1664 and 1665, people flocked outdoors in their tens of thousands to view this new presage which was a much more brilliant object than any comet seen in living memory. Its dominant presence in the night skies all over Europe caused consternation in those who still believed comets were harbingers of evil. One German scholar wrote: 'I tremble when I recall the terrible appearance it had on Saturday evening in the clear sky, when it was observed by every-body with inexpressible astonishment. It seems as though the heavens were burning, or as if the very air were on fire . . . from this little star stretched out such a wonderfully long tail even an intellectual man was overcome with trembling; one's hair stood on end as this uncommon, terrible, and indescribable tail came into view.'

Some people thought the comet's influence *more* powerful. One story related that in Rome a hen much disturbed by the apparition had laid eggs on which were imprinted the image of the visitor and other significant celestial signs. Those who doubted that such things could happen stared in wonder when they later saw it reproduced in a book. In Germany comet medallions were struck, engraved with the dire message 'This star threatens evil things. Trust in God, who will turn them to good'.

Halley and his companion Nelson were two of the first people to catch sight of the 'new' comet when it re-emerged into the twilight sky. The pair of youthful travellers had just made a very rough crossing of the English Channel and were pressing on by coach to Paris. Now, after sighting the 'new' brilliant comet with its splendid tail, they were anxious to make contact with Giovanni Cassini (1625-1712), Director of the Paris Observatory, to whom Halley had a letter of introduction.

Meantime, back at Trinity College, Cambridge, Newton was himself busy observing the new comet with the same zeal he had applied to the comet of 1664. At first he noted its daily shifts with the naked eye, but because he was short-sighted, he tried a monocle which he found made the comet much more distinct.

He had followed the 'first' comet since early November 1680, shortly after it had become visible in the dawn sky and then he tracked it on every clear morning thereafter until it disappeared towards the Sun's rays. Two weeks later he had quickly picked up the new, even more brilliant, comet in the early evening sky. This second comet was apparently moving *away* from the Sun in contrast to the first. Not until Flamsteed raised the possibility does it seem to have occurred to Newton that the two comets might be one and the same.

Comets fascinated Newton. He had in his mind the seed of a grand theory – grander and more comprehensive than Kepler had envisaged for his universal laws governing the movements of heavenly bodies. How did comets fit these laws? Kepler had believed comets were outside them; Newton suspected Kepler was wrong in his assumption. Meanwhile he would secure as many observations of comets as he could muster, for these would provide the basic data to work upon for his theory – just as Kepler had used Tycho Brahe's observations of the planets to discover the three basic laws.

Newton continued to watch with his monocle until the new comet faded and was no longer distinct. Then he switched to a telescope of three-foot focal length. A week later the comet had grown much dimmer and a more powerful instrument was required. Now he chose a telescope of seven-foot focal length in which the eyepiece was equipped with a micrometer so he could measure the angular offsets of the head of the comet against the background stars; these observations would one day help him compute its exact path.

By 11 February (Old Style calendar) the comet had become so faint that Newton was unable to find it. Nevertheless, he now had a fair idea of its day-to-day shifts across the backcloth of stars and so he kept up his vigil along its predicted track. On 9 March (OS) he at last succeeded in glimpsing it again. Newton was probably the last observer on Earth to see the great comet – now having retreated so far from the Sun it had long ago lost its tail. In modern times the comet of 1680 has frequently been called Newton's comet because of his comprehensive work in attempting to solve its orbit when he came to write *Principia* a few years later.

As soon as they reached Paris, Halley and Nelson introduced themselves to Cassini at the Observatory. The French astronomer had already heard of Halley's growing reputation and offered him open hospitality and the opportunity to make use of all the instruments at the Observatory as often as he wished.

Ensconced in Paris, Halley regularly corresponded with his friends back at the Royal Society. Hooke had requested him to look out for some scientific books, difficult to obtain in London, and Flamsteed, who apparently was still on speaking terms with his one-time protégé, had asked him to purchase for him a new map of the Moon.

In his first letter to Hooke, Halley tells him: '. . . the general talk of the virtuosi here is about the Comet . . .' Then in a later letter says: '. . . Monseur Cassini did me the favour to give me his books of ye Comett Just as I was goeing out of towne . . . he has given a theory of its motion wch. is, that this Comet was the same with that appeared to Tycho Anno 1577, that it performes its revolution round the Sun in a great Circle including the earth. wch. he will have to be fixt in about 2 yeares and halfe . . .'

Halley remarks to Hooke that it may be difficult for him to accept the idea but intimates that he himself has a sneaking regard for it. Using his own observations, Halley attempted to reconcile the comet's movement with the old idea of constant rectilinear motion, but found (not surprisingly) this was unsatisfactory. Some of Cassini's ideas were unfortunately to colour Halley's thinking for a long time and handicap him in his own ambitions to solve the problem about the paths in which comets moved.

But comets were only one of Halley's many wide-ranging interests in Paris. Everything was grist to his mill. Nothing went to waste, and years later he was using basic data picked up during his stay in the city.

He made a deep impression on the French savants. Generations later the French astronomer François Arago (1786-1853), who served as director at the Paris Observatory, recalled that the young English astronomer was remembered as 'a charming man of rare intelligence'.

After Paris, Halley and Nelson toured various parts of France and then headed for Rome where Halley busied himself enquiring about the Greek and Roman foot standards and visiting antiquities. It was in November 1681 that he received a disturbing letter which necessitated he give up the tour and return to London.

What precisely was in this letter is unknown. It is generally supposed it concerned his father's rapidly dwindling fortunes which had first taken a setback with the destruction of family property during the Great Fire of 1666. Halley's mother had died in 1672, and while his father remarried, it is not known at what date this occurred. It has been conjectured that under pressure from his stepmother, or stepmother-to-be, Halley's father was forced to cut his elder son's generous allowance. Certainly there is ample evidence that Halley disliked his stepmother, and in later years he took her to court to protect the remains of his patrimony.

The prospect of insufficient funds to continue his jaunt in Europe and the even grimmer prospects of soon having to find a situation to support himself may have initially panicked Halley into action. However, he didn't appear to have returned to London post haste and he eventually reached England via Holland on 24 January 1682.

Nelson remained behind in Italy. In Rome he had met and fallen in love with Lady Theophile Lucy, a wealthy widow and the daughter of the Earl of Berkeley, and the pair were married soon after.

We hear little more of Nelson in Halley's shadowy life. However, there can be no doubt the two remained firm friends, and a surviving letter gleaned from the Nelson correspondence confirms this. Nevertheless, we should like to hear more about Halley's close friendship with Nelson if for no other reason than Nelson was strongly religious and had influence with the bishops while Halley a few years hence had earned the reputation of a heretic and was debarred from a professorship at Oxford because of his supposed irreligious views.

With romance and money in the air, it is perhaps no surprise to find Halley emulating the example of his friend Nelson within three months of his return to London. Again the documentation of his life at this period is extremely sketchy. We only know the date of his return from Italy because it occurs as a short note in Hooke's diary. Whatever happened in the interim, Halley's marriage to a Mary Tooke was solemnized on 20 April 1682.

Very little is known about Mary Tooke and her family. Traditionally she is always described by Halley's previous biographers as the daughter of the Auditor of the Exchequer. However, this does not seem to agree with the facts. Between 1673-98 Sir Robert Howard (1626-98) – Dryden's brother-in-law – supposedly held this office and either side of these dates no Tooke (Took or Tuke – the contemporary spellings vary) is recorded.[3]

Outwardly there was no reason for the couple's haste in the marriage; at least the first official child was not born until several years later. Whether Halley knew Mary Tooke before leaving for his grand tour is unknown. Unknown too are the circumstances of their first meeting. There is a strong possibility the marriage was a highly romantic, runaway affair. A clue to this is that the ceremony took place at St James's Church, near Aldgate, an establishment famous at the time for several other rapidly executed marriages where couples were not required to wait for a reading of banns or a licence.

If it was a runaway marriage, it is legitimate to speculate on the possible reasons for it. Halley was a young man without immediate prospects. If his allowance had been cut to the bone owing to failing family fortunes, he needed to find a new source to support himself while making his way in the scientific world. A wife with a dowry – an income? – might just be the stopgap which appealed to him. He would not be the first impecunious young man to have decided a fortuitous marriage was the best way to solve a temporary financial difficulty. We can imagine the misgivings of the bride's parents. The bride's father, whether in the Auditor's Office of the Exchequer or a merchant, was a man to whom money was a way of life. Did he and his wife recognize the young astronomer as an adventurer – a suitor after their daughter's dowry? Worse still, did the bride's parents get a whiff of the coffee-house gossip surrounding the potential bridegroom's wild-oats adventures in St Helena and Danzig?

Mary Tooke almost certainly brought money to the marriage, otherwise it is difficult to see how Halley maintained his lifestyle in the early years of the marriage and where, five years later, he conjured up the funds to print and publish at his own personal expense Newton's *Principia*. It was not from his small salary as Clerk to the Royal Society, a minor position he was appointed to in 1684, as we know he was never paid his very modest stipend in hard cash.

Whatever the circumstances of Halley's betrothal to Mary Tooke, it was an out-and-out love match that spanned fifty-four years of contented married life. Shortly after her marriage Mary Tooke was described by a friend of Halley as 'a young lady amiable for the gracefullness of her person & the beauties of her mind'. By Halley's own admission it was one of the saddest days of his life when his wife died in 1736.

After their marriage in 1682, the young couple settled in Islington, then a fast-growing country village north of the City. In Islington the sky was free of the smoke pollution then rapidly overtaking London. Halley set up his telescope and sextant in a small observatory and began a long-term programme observing the Moon's motion over a cycle of eighteen years – a period known since the early Babylonians whereby the Moon goes through a series of gyrations in its path round the Earth. The Moon's irregular motion during this eighteen-year cycle was a problem that interested Halley all his life as it also interested Newton. Like the problem of the comets it had intrigued many astronomers. Any man who could shed light on the slightly erratic nature of the Moon's shifts and explain them mathematically would win lasting fame and bring benefit to mariners in helping them determine accurate longitude at sea. The explanation of the Moon's motion was one of the few problems in astronomy that had immediate economic interest to the community at large and it was this, and the general problem of timekeeping, which was the chief motivation of Charles II in establishing the Royal Greenwich Observatory in 1675.

While their mutual interests in comets were to bring Halley and Newton into a close accord, their mutual, but independent, interests in solving the Moon's motion were to culminate in an open discord during the last days of Newton's life and cause Thomas Hearne – never a friend of Halley – to blame him for hastening Newton's end.

In Islington, Halley apparently soon settled down to domestic routine and was an attentive husband, but Martin Foulkes (1690-1754), who knew Halley well in his latter years, tells us briefly 'neither the domestic cares, nor joys of a happy marriage could diminish his ardour for astronomy & science'.

Halley's ardours, nevertheless, were by no means limited to heavenly matters, and during the course of his marriage he fathered one son and two daughters.

A few months after settling in Islington, destiny for the young astronomer came calling in the form of yet another bright comet. It arrived in August 1682 about the time William Penn, a friend of Halley at the Royal Society, set sail to found the new Pennsylvania Colony. Flamsteed observed the new comet from Greenwich, Newton from Cambridge and Halley from his recently erected domestic observatory in Islington. Not so brilliant as the comet he had seen on the road to Paris at the start of his grand tour, it, nevertheless, greatly interested Halley as well as Newton and Flamsteed, and the trio independently made careful observations of its slow shifts across the backcloth of stars.

Newton, for some time, had again been quietly researching the problem of cometary paths. Now the advent of the new comet in 1682 made him more determined to pursue the problem to the end. Halley was involving himself in all manner of diverse problems. He was still busy establishing his position as a virtuoso of the first rank – a cut above the dabblers in science who made up most of the Royal Society fellowship. His interests ranged from the satellites of Saturn to variations of 'the magnetical compass'. Ironically it was his work in magnetism (nowadays the Earth science of geophysics) which was to make him best remembered in his own lifetime and in the immediate years following rather than his astronomical discoveries – including those about the orbit of the 1682 comet . . .

Sometime in late 1682 it came to Newton's notice that Halley had made a series of observations of the new comet as well as of the 1680-1 comet. Newton wrote to Halley discussing these observations as he wished to use them in his own researches. The upshot was that the two met; the circumstances are not known, but it was probably in London in the rooms of the Royal Society at Gresham College in Bishopsgate, just inside the City's old Roman walls.

Halley had given little further thought to the comets whose positions he had observed; while comets per se interested him, interest in the orbit of the comet linked with his own destiny was temporarily pushed aside as at this time he was casting his mind round to see how he might gain new insights into more general matters astronomical.

It was in the spring of 1684 that his active mind turned its attention to the three famous laws of planetary motion formulated by Kepler earlier in the century. Halley was puzzled about certain consequences following on from these laws. For example, he wondered why it was that the time taken by a planet to travel round the Sun should *always* relate to the ratio 2:3 as in the third law.

Soon Halley concluded that this ratio might be due to the Sun attracting each planet with an influence, or force, that depended on the *inverse square of the distance between the Sun and the particular planet* – or, in other words, an influence, or force, which diminshed by *four* times if the distance were doubled or *nine* times if the distance were trebled.

Halley's reasoning had provided him with an insight into how gravity worked at distance in space; excited by this new knowledge, he decided in January 1684 to discuss it with Hooke at the Royal Society. Also present at the discussion was Sir Christopher Wren. To Halley's and Wren's surprise, Hooke immediately claimed to have been working along the same lines of thought for some time. In addition, he boasted he had worked out a geometrical proof of it – something that Halley readily admitted he had been unable to do, hence his decision to consult with Hooke as a man of wider experience.

Hooke, now eagerly pressed by Halley and Wren to reveal this geometrical proof, declined the invitation. Wren, immediately suspicious of Hooke's glib off-the-cuff claim, decided to put him to the test. He long knew from his own experience about Hooke's sometime braggadocio style. He and Hooke had been colleagues for many years in helping replan and then rebuild London after the Great Fire. Hooke was often too ready to claim for himself what was beyond his particular genius to solve. Wren knew Hooke to be weak in mathematics – much weaker than himself, and the problem that young Halley had independently stumbled upon had been on his own mind and on that of others in the past, yet none of them had been able to take it a stage further.

Wren realized Halley was a good mathematician, equal, if not superior, to himself. This was an opportunity to stretch him as well as call Hooke's bluff: if either Hooke or Halley could prove the proposition, he would present the first to submit it for scrutiny with the gift of a book of his own choice to the value of forty shillings.

The reward itself was a trifle. Wren meant it to be, but it was a direct shot across Hooke's bows. Wren had called his bluff: Put up or shut up! The time-limit for claiming the prize was two months.

In the weeks following, Halley tried hard to solve the problem but finally admitted to Wren it defeated him. It was now time for Hooke to respond, and Wren and Halley taxed him about it. Hooke, realizing Halley's own failure, decided to play for more time. He told the pair he had decided to keep his own proof a secret until others had a chance to work it out; by doing this they would value the solution more when he presented it!

Halley was too proud to let the problem defeat him. He now knew that neither Wren nor any other mathematician in London could help him, but perhaps he did know one man in Cambridge who might just be able to. It would give him a chance to renew his acquaintance with this strange, aloof, but brilliant scholar who had enquired about his comet observations but who rarely came to London. The more he thought about it, the more he became convinced Isaac Newton was just the man to help him . . .

Notes

[1] How exactly Halley pronounced his name is uncertain. While the Halleys of today seem to favour Hali or Haili, in Pepys's naval minutes the name is sometimes written Hawley. However, in tune with the inexact spelling of the age, we find in seventeenth and eighteenth-century records several alternative renderings including: Hailey, Hayley, Haley, Haly and Hally. There is evidence that some British eighteenth-century Halleys who settled in Virginia, USA, used the pronounciation Hawley.

[2] Thomas Hearne (1678-1735) was an antiquarian and a prolific author. He held the position of second keeper at the Bodleian Library but was forced to resign in 1716 owing to his Jacobite sympathies. He knew Halley extremely well; part of his dislike of the astronomer stemmed from Halley's, apparently oft-repeated, condemnation of Mary Queen of Scots.

[3] By coincidence Sir Robert Howard had a daughter named Mary by one of his four marriages, but she is not the personage of this mystery. While the *Dictionary of National Biography* (1908) records Halley's bride as 'Mary, daughter of Mr Tooke, auditor of the exchequer', Bernard Fontenelle, Halley's contemporary and sometime acquaintance, who was responsible for the version of Halley's biography which appeared in two episodes in the *Gentleman's Magazine* in 1747 (*see Biographical note*), refers to her specifically as 'Mrs Mary Tooke'. Assuming he knew the true facts, it raises the possibility that Halley married a moneyed widow (as his friend Nelson did), and this may explain where Halley derived his principal living expenses, apart from any remaining patrimony. Even so, this is not conclusive for unmarried ladies of the period were addressed as 'Mrs'. . .

There were several well-to-do families of Tooke (and its variant spellings) living in London at the time. Whether one of these was employed as a subordinate to Howard is a possibility; alternatively he might have been auditor for some other government office. However, one Tooke at least was a well-known poulterer, and it is significant that Halley among his many accomplishments was remarkably knowledgeable about poultry. Eugene

Fairfield MacPike in his source-book of Halleiana (*see Biographical note*) records that by marriage of a first cousin in 1696, Halley became related to some poulterers 'with whom he may have been previously acquainted'. In extracts referring to Halley from the Journal Books of the Royal Society we read that on 27 November 1689, Halley lectured the Society about 'the way that Poultrers knew whether wild-fowl is fresh, or no, is by the foot, for they conclude, that the foot being dry is certain, they are stale, if not, they are esteemed fresh'. It is apparent that Halley by this time had 'inside' knowledge of the trade and he may have derived this from his marriage to Mary Tooke.

3 · 'Halley's Book'

ALLEY MENTIONS his visit to Newton in Cambridge in August 1684 in a letter written some years later, but the best account of the historic meeting comes second-hand via the recollections recounted by Newton's close friend the French-born mathematician Abraham De Moivre (1667-1754).

We are told: 'In 1684 Dr Halley came to visit him [Newton] at Cambridge, after they had been some time together, the Dr asked him what he thought the Curve would be that would be described by the Planets supposing the force towards the Sun to be reciprocal to the square of their distances from it. Sr Isaac replied immediately that it would be an Ellipsis, the Doctor struck with joy & amazement asked him how he knew it, why saith he I have calculated it whereupon Dr Halley asked him for his calculation without any farther delay, Sr Isaac looked among his papers but could not find it, but he promised him to renew it, & then send it him.'

Halley had no reason to suspect that Newton was bluffing as Hooke had been. He had already formed an opinion that the man fourteen years his senior was someone of unique mathematical talents. Newton, on his part, had been purposely cautious with Halley. He was not yet sure of Halley's real motives for coming to see him in Cambridge. Halley, after all, was on familiar terms with Hooke – the man he himself despised most of all.

The fact that Newton had taken a bitter dislike to Hooke after he had criticised the Theory of Colours and again a few years back when Hooke had tried to open up a correspondence with him made Newton hesitate to be entirely open with anyone who belonged to Hooke's immediate circle at the Royal Society . . .

There is good reason to believe that Newton was not strictly telling the truth in the assertion he had mislaid his proof. Because in some earlier correspondence Hooke had caught him out in an elementary blunder and then practically ridiculed him before the eyes of his peers at the Royal Society, it made him think twice about showing it to Halley. The story goes Newton was soon to be grateful he had heeded caution. After Halley had departed for London, Newton decided to recheck his claimed demonstration, but this time it did not work out! However, it was only carelessness again. A hastily drawn diagram had led him to confuse a geometric figure. In due course, by burning the midnight oil, he arrived at the correct solution . . .

Halley received Newton's proof two months later via the hand of a third party. When Halley read it, he was astounded. There was apparently good reason for the delay. It was not just the proof to the problem they had discussed during his visit but a complete treatise consisting of nine pages, titled in Latin *De motu corporum in gyrum* (*On the Motion of Bodies in an Orbit*). As a mathematician of considerable talent himself, Halley was overwhelmed by the sheer brilliance of Newton's treatment. It confirmed his previous suspicions that Newton was a man whose powers knew few equals.

The treatment demonstrated not only Kepler's third law but the other two as well. It fell short of a complete solution to planetary motions, but Halley recognized it as the greatest leap forward since Kepler's work.

After digesting *De motu*, Halley made a second trip to Cambridge on 10 December 1684 to personally congratulate Newton on his accomplishment. The outcome was that Halley persuaded Newton to write a book and expand the ideas contained in the nine pages.

Newton was certainly flattered by Halley's attention and his unreserved encouragement. He now appreciated that the young astronomer was no acolyte of Hooke bent on mischief. He readily agreed he would compose a tract entitled *De motu corporum* (*The Motion of Bodies*). It was a work to occupy him to the exclusion of all else for eighteen months . . .

*   *   *

Gravity was no new force discovered by Isaac Newton. The idea of a force acting on the Earth and planetary bodies had been around for some time before. While Kepler had discovered the three basic laws *describing* the movements of the planets, he had not exploited these formulations to explain *why* a planet continues to revolve round the Sun and *why* it does not fly off into space.

The main question raised by Kepler's work and left unanswered was why the planets described elliptical paths in preference to all other types of path.

Galileo had refuted the Aristotelian doctrine of differently weighted bodies falling at different speeds and provided insights as to *how gravity worked on Earth*. He even foreshadowed two of Newton's laws of motion. He showed how rectilinear – straight-line – motion of a cannon-ball projected horizontally changes into curvilinear motion. He demonstrated that it was the Earth's gravity which caused the cannon-ball to fall towards the Earth and in doing so it traced out the curve of a parabola, which is nothing more than an ellipse whose major axis is infinitely long. However, much like Kepler's, Galileo's vision and insights were limited by the acceptance of medieval dogma.

It was clear to all who followed Galileo and Kepler that all heavy bodies were in some way attracted by the Earth from the experimental fact that every body falling freely sought the Earth's centre. But *how* a central force lodged inside the Earth (or the Sun) could operate to keep up a motion of revolution in distant bodies round any centre was one of God's remaining inexplicable mysteries.

The ancients had noted that when a stone in a sling was whirled rapidly, a force was developed which stretched the string by which the stone is held. Christiaan Huygens (1629-93), more a physicist than an astronomer, defined this as *centrifugal* force, and it came to be accepted that this was the key to the problem. Thus a tendency to fly from the centre had to be generated, and therefore in the planets and their satellites this tendency must exist.

In about 1666 the Italian mathematician-cum-physician Giovanni Alfonso Borelli (1608-79) seems to have grasped the fact that the elliptical paths of the planets round the Sun and the similar paths of the satellites round their primaries might be due to two forces present which mutually destroy or counterbalance each other and leave the planet or satellite in a state of dynamical equilibrium to pursue its journey round the Sun or parent body. Indeed, Borelli's idea was the germ of universal gravitation.

Borelli, however, like Hooke a few years later when he followed up similar ideas, was unable to demonstrate these counterbalancing forces mathematically. It was an apt descriptive idea, but no more than that.

Newton was to give Borelli generous credit as one of his predecessors by whom he profited.

Gravity itself remained an enigma. While it existed in the Earth and was likely in other cosmic bodies, it was an intangible force and could only be visualized second-hand from its effect on other bodies. Kepler had believed gravity was somehow a magnetic force. Flamsteed, drawing on similar ideas, had used it to explain why the two comets in 1680-1 were actually the same – first by invoking its attraction towards the Sun (on its inward path) then its repulsion (on its outward path). While Kepler was right when he described gravity as a 'mutual corporeal affection between cognate bodies', he got no nearer to explaining how it was the primary driving mechanism for the cosmos.

However, the planets and satellites must be held in place by some mechanism, and in the interim between Kepler and Halley and Newton the vacuum of thought was filled by invoking the system of vortices elaborated by René Descartes (1596-1650).

What Descartes put forward was an ingenious solution to the problem, but still medieval in concept. He believed planets to be dead stars revolving in a material vortex, kept in their orbits by the pressure of nearby vortices, and terrestrial gravity was deemed to be 'the reaction exerted upon gross bodies by more volatile particles revolving rapidly in a secondary vortex that encompassed the Earth and having the same axis of the Earth'.

Descartes had grasped the idea of inertia (i.e. the tendency of matter to remain at rest or keep moving in the same direction – unless affected by some outside force) later to be incorporated by Newton into his first law.

Others following elaborated on Descartes's theory – known as Cartesianism – including Huygens, but its days were numbered when Newton began to put together his great synthesis.

Newton rejected the tenets of Cartesian philosophy soon after thinking about gravity when the Plague closed down Cambridge University in 1665-6 and he returned temporarily to his native Woolsthorpe. Until Halley arrived in Cambridge that fateful August day in 1684, nearly twenty years later, Newton had intermittently been pursuing the problems of gravity and celestial motion. During the interim his mind was roving over other significant problems in mathematics, alchemy, optics, theology and biblical chronology. His notions about universal gravity did not all spring from the much publicized event of his watching the apple fall in the orchard while at Woolsthorpe. However, this seems to have channelled his thinking in how the Earth pulled at the Moon and in turn the Moon pulled at the Earth to create a dynamical stability between them. The falling-apple story is apparently true enough and no anecdote invented by a past biographer to colour and leaven an otherwise abstruse subject. But Newton's laws took several years to work out and detail into shape. The process involved him in thousands of hours of thought drudgery; several of the key concepts later published in *Principia* had remained for years at the border of his consciousness as fleeting ideas not yet properly grasped. The commitment he had entered into with Halley to write a book was his way to come to grips with these ideas and resolve them in hard print. It was an enormous challenge to his own self-esteem. One driving-force was the constant thought that if he brought it off, he would best his old enemy Hooke; this was the sauce that flavoured the otherwise dreary meal of eighteen months' intellectual labour.

How much Newton knew of Hooke's own investigations which parallelled his own is not clear. Hooke quite independently had been on the right track. Since about 1666 he had realized that a planet moving in its orbit is under a constant force pulling it sunwards. He knew this was the reason a planet does not move off in a straight line into outer space. By 1670, Hooke had also come to realize the force exerted by the Sun was linked with terrestrial gravity. Even earlier he had tried to establish by experiment that the Earth's force of gravity decreased with increasing height above the Earth' surface, which of course it does. This led him to adopt the hypothesis based on Kepler's third law that gravitational attraction varied inversely as the square of the distance from the attracting body. Thus, Hooke comprehended, gravity was a cosmic force not limited to the Earth. Nevertheless, proving mathematically *how* a planet, moving in an elliptical orbit, was held by the Sun was another matter. This was his stumbling-block. His pride was such he could not bring himself to admit to his peers at the Royal Society that the problem had defeated him.

Following Halley's second visit to Cambridge in December 1684, Newton became totally immersed in his book. According to his own statement when he started he had no conception where his pursuit would lead him.

Comets were to figure in his book. The problem of cometary motion he knew was a harder nut to crack than the motions of the planets. After observing the 1680-1 comet, and before the appearance of the 1682 (later Halley's) comet, he was already working hard trying to solve the dynamics of its path, applying a method he had evolved using four separate observations. He was corresponding with Flamsteed about his method and still unconvinced that the second comet of 1680 was the first returning in a different guise. Distrust of Flamsteed's magnetic theory for the movements of comets – first being attracted towards the Sun by one pole (of the comet) and then repelled by the other opposite pole – led him to discard any of Flamsteed's ideas of the single identity of the two comets.

Newton's surviving papers seem to indicate he had solved the mechanics of planetary motion in about 1679, but at that time he had no accurate observations he could apply to any comets to see if they might follow the same principles. After the 1680-1 comet, he wrote to Flamsteed telling him he was now trying to reconcile the new comet with the dynamical principles of planetary motion. Even so, he was not yet emancipated from the old arguments about rectilinear paths for comets, and Halley at this time was also having the same trouble. By 1682, however, Newton had made the break and now accepted that comet orbits *must* be curved ones. He had not the slightest inkling that two years earlier Georg Samuel Dörfell, an obscure Protestant clergyman from Saxony and ex-pupil of Hevelius, had published a small book consisting of five leaves in quarto and one woodcut on which are represented parabolic orbits for comets. It is doubtful if Newton or Halley ever saw the book in their lifetimes or ever heard the name of its author, and Dörfell's ideas had absolutely no influence on either Englishman. Today his small book is a very rare collectors' item.

The impact of Newton's nine-page *De motu* on Royal Society fellows was limited simply because few had been able to understand it. Even Flamsteed was puzzled by it, and initially it was probably only Halley who could recognize its true significance. Even before submitting it to Halley, Newton seems to have been covertly planning the longer work which Halley on his visit of 10 December 1684, not surprisingly, now found him agreeable to write. *De motu* was a cautious digest of his ideas to test the intellectual temperature. Halley's glowing praise was just the kind of response he had been waiting for, rebuff would have been fatal. Halley was the catalyst that both emotionally and materially brought *Principia* to life. Even during the time Halley was circulating 'a curious treatise De motu', Newton was busy writing to Flamsteed requesting new observational data to allow him to make his demonstrations more precise for the longer work. He told him: 'Now I am upon this subject I would gladly know ye bottom of it before I publish my papers . . .'

In getting to the bottom of it the effort absorbed his waking hours for a year and a half, and what lectures he gave to students were thinly disguised drafts of his embryo book!

During this time those who knew him at Cambridge noted his highly erratic behaviour. While walking through the college or street of the town, he was perpetually self-absorbed; he would often suddenly stop and then hurry back to his rooms to jot down a new thought which had just occurred to him. At other times his preoccupation with ideas would cause him to take a wrong direction and he would find himself not at the destination he had first intended when he set out.

Some of his enquiries to Flamsteed requested information about the coordinates of two stars in Perseus near which the 1680-1 comet had passed. He told Flamsteed: 'I do intend to determin ye lines described by ye comets of 1664 & 1680 according to ye principles observed by ye Planets . . .' Had Newton decided to extend the scope of his investigation to a study of the comet of 1682, he might well have deprived Halley of his own prize when in the decade following publication of *Principia* he discovered the true periodicity of it.

In *De motu*, Newton had drawn upon a lesson in circular motion taught him by Hooke during some correspondence between them in 1679. Stemming from this Newton introduced a new word into the accepted vocabulary of mechanics: 'I call that by which a body is impelled or attracted towards some point which is regarded as a centre centripetal force.' He afterwards explained he had coined the word 'centripetal' − seeking the centre − in a deliberate parallel to the word 'centrifugal' − fleeing the centre − invented by Christiaan Huygens not long before. Centrifugal and centripetal forces were the very two counterbalancing forces Borelli had declared brought about the stability of planets in their orbits round the Sun. Of course, Borelli did not know them by those names. It was the investigation of centripetal forces as they determine orbital motion which characterized Newton's contribution to universal gravitation in *Principia*.

During the longer work Newton was in touch with Halley, keeping him informed of progress and about new insights. Some of the original *De motu* underwent several revisions. Newton was an author who chose to develop ideas by committing himself to writing several successive drafts. Each contained steps forward in his thinking over the previous one. In one letter he wrote to Halley he remarked: '. . . gravity is one kind of centripetal force. My calculations reveal that the centripetal force by which our Moon is held in her monthly orbit round the Earth is to the force of gravity at the surface of the Earth very nearly as the reciprocal of the square of the distance from the centre of the Earth.' Whereas Newton's predecessors had only invented descriptive theories, his genius was such he was able to dress out his ideas in concrete numbers.

His plan was to divide his treatise into three Books. Comets were providing him with the hardest nut to crack. On 20 June 1686 he confided to Halley his theory of comets still remained unfinished: '. . . In Autumn last I spent two months in calculations to no purpose for want of a good method wch made me afterwards return to ye first Book & enlarge it with diverse Propositions some relating to comets.'

It was in Book II Newton set down his ideas that comets definitely come under the same laws of orbital motion he had formulated for planets, concluding: '. . . Therefore, during the whole time of their appearance, comets fall within the sphere of activity of the circumsolar force, and are acted upon by its impulse & therefore describe conic sections that have their foci in the centre of the Sun, and by radii drawn to the Sun describe areas proportional to the times [as per Kepler's third law]. For that force, propagated to an immense distance, will govern the motion of bodies far beyond the orbit of Saturn [then the farthest planet known].'

However, Newton was still vexed he was unable to work out a practical method and provide an example of a particular comet's movements as he could calculate for the planets and the Moon. The truth is, Newton never did quite succeed in applying his method to a particular comet. Perhaps in this instance the Fates were against him when he chose the example of the 1680-1 comet to demonstrate his hit-and-miss method in *Principia*. Had he chosen the 1682 comet, the story of Newton and Halley might have been very different.

Newton meantime relied on Halley to provide him with criticism on his successive drafts. Newton by now had recognized that Halley was one of the few men in Europe to whom he could turn in confidence and seek advice. He was working beyond the established frontiers of science and needed someone with an intellect comparable with his own to use as a sounding-board and keep him in check; someone sympathetic to the problems of a scholar working in isolation.

It needed someone of Halley's tact to tread warily through this potential minefield. The young astronomer realized one false step, and the fruits of *Principia* might wither unharvested and remain lost to the world outside Newton's mind.

Some of Halley's suggestions Newton adopted. We know this because of his preoccupation with preserving every draft of his work in progress, and the alterations survive among Newton's papers to this day.

As the work was nearing its end, it must have been sweet music to Newton's ears when Halley in his replies to letters waxed lyrical and referred to 'your divine Treatise', adding the ultimate accolade 'Nearer the gods no mortal may approach'.

*   *   *

Since his second trip to Cambridge in December 1684 to persuade Newton to expand *De motu* into a longer work, Halley's own career had taken off at a tangent. Back in March 1684, Halley's father – another Edmond – died in mysterious circumstances. The story goes he left his house telling his (second) wife he would be back by evening. He was not seen alive again.

All knowledge of this incident is derived from a broadsheet published about 17 April entitled 'A true Discovery of Mr Edmund Halley of London Merchant When was found Barborously Murthered at Temple-Farm, near Rochester in Kent.'

Whether it was actual murder or suicide remains conjectural. Halley's earlier biographers working from the same sources differ in opinion. Bizarre gossip in later years was to link the astronomer's name with his own father's death. Again Thomas Hearne is a source of this innuendo when he wrote 'Dr Halley's Father went in fear of his life from his own Son'.

While this accusation is malicious, it is highly probable that relations between father and son were strained after Halley senior's remarriage. Following his return from the grand tour, Halley's patrimonial sources of income were greatly reduced. We might suppose the family's declining soapboiling business, combined with a curb by the second wife on the purse-strings of a once over-indulgent father, may have led to a family dispute.

After his father's death, Halley's stepmother married again and reappeared as either Mrs Chester or Cleator – the name is written unclearly in the records. Halley senior died intestate, and ten years after his death, Edmond junior took his ex-stepmother to court to protect some remaining interests. However, there are few details and no information about what monies or property were involved.

Meanwhile, in 1685, the astronomer, except for his wife's income or dowry, was apparently without significant financial resources. Whatever the true circumstances of Halley's personal fortunes, and these are by no means clear from the record, he was an eager applicant for the post of Clerkship to the Royal Society when this new appointment arose. We can only conclude that because the post carried a stipend of £50 per annum, by no means a generous sum even for those days, he made application. If not for financial reasons – for what else? Why would he sacrifice his honoured status as a virtuoso 'gentleman' and accept that of a paid employee, since it was laid down in the Statutes of the Society that no paid employee could hold membership as a Fellow. It must have been a trying time for an up-and-coming young man, once of independent means in receipt of an allowance of £300 per annum, to accept paid employment and doubtless loss of face with his peers.

Nevertheless, it seems other fellows also applied for the new vacancy, and the voting went to a second ballot. This was held on 27 January 1686 when Halley secured a majority and was then sworn into office. A condition of employment for the new Clerk was that he should be a bachelor and live at the Royal Society's meeting place at Gresham College. This, however, was waived in Halley's favour because the previous year the young couple had already moved house from Islington to Golden Lion Court in Aldersgate Street so they could be nearer their City friends and the Royal Society premises.

*   *   *

In April 1686, Newton's Book I was delivered to the Royal Society, and Halley as Clerk made a report to the Council. Again events are hazy, but on 19 May the Society ordered 'Mr Newton's *Philosophiae naturalis principia mathematica* be printed forthwith in quarto and in fair letter . . . that a letter be written to him [Newton] to signify the society's resolution and to desire his opinion to the print, volume cuts, & etc'.

All along Halley had been the driving force in the production of Newton's book. In his role as Clerk to the Society he constantly used his influence to promote the project. Now, suddenly, the full responsibility of underwriting its printing fell into his private lap. Why this occurred and where he found the money to do it is not known. He probably used his wife's money. The Society itself was constantly short of funds. So far, as Clerk, he had not even been paid his promised £50 stipend.

Sitting in the presidential chair at this time was Samuel Pepys. He had allowed his membership to lapse in the mid-1660s, but John Evelyn begged him to come back in 1680 when the Society was in low water and needed eminent public figures and some influential men of affairs to bolster its image. The Society did pick up and was soon making more stringent rules about conditions for admission. Pepys was made President in 1686 and was still in office when the first part of the manuscript for *Principia* arrived.

Shortly before, the Society had printed Francis Willughby's *History of Fishes*. It was a work dedicated to Pepys because he had dipped generously

54

into his own pocket to pay for 79 of the 187 plates. The rest were covered by contributions of twenty other fellows. Five hundred copies were printed and priced at £1.5s on ordinary paper and £1.8s on best paper. The book was a commercial disaster; and there were still unsold copies as late as 1743. With its fingers burnt with this previous undertaking, the Society would not risk underwriting Newton's work no matter how brilliantly its new Clerk waxed forth about it. Anyway, most of the Society's fellowship suspected Newton's very abstract book, that few of them could understand, would follow the same fate as Willughby's. Whatever the circumstances, and these are not clear, Newton's book went ahead. Halley as Clerk had more or less promised Newton the Society would foot the printing-bill. It is possible that when Council vetoed this, Halley, having fathered the book and feeling the responsibility, was committed morally to seeing it through and so carried the financial burden himself. There is certainly no record of Halley approaching Newton or anyone else to help out.

The Society remained so short of funds Halley's £50 stipend remained unpaid. In lieu of it, Council voted to give him fifty copies of the fish book! Halley's reaction to this generous decision is unknown. He probably accepted it philosophically. He likely took his fifty copies and disposed of them for cash to Samuel Smith, a well-known bookseller, printer and remainder-merchant of the day whose premises were in St Paul's Churchyard. In November 1688, while William of Orange was quietly invading England, the Council ordered Halley (probably on his own recommendation) to see if he could arrange a bargain with the same Samuel Smith for disposal of another considerable parcel of 'the Book de Piscibus'.

*   *   *

It was during the initial stages of the production of *Principia* that a dark cloud appeared on Newton's horizon. This was related to some information contained in a letter from Halley in London; in the same letter he told Newton he had officially been placed in charge of publication by the Society. After discussing some suggested changes in diagrams, Halley raised his other news from London as tactfully as possible. In doing so he explained he was personally disturbed on Newton's behalf as his confidant and friend but: '. . . I ought to informe you of, viz that Mr Hook has some pretensions upon the invention of ye role of the decrease of Gravity, being reciprocally as the squares of the distance from the centre. He sais you had the notion from him, though he owns the Demonstration of the Curves generated thereby to be wholly your own; how much this is so, you know best, as likewise what you have to do in this matter, only Mr Hook seems to expect you should make some mention of him in the preface, which, it is possible, you may see reason to praefix. I must beg your pardon that is I, that send you this account, but I thought it my duty to let you know it, that so you may act accordingly; being in myself fully satisfied, that nothing but the greatest candour imaginable, is to be expected from a person, who of all men has the least need to borrow reputation.'

It must have been a difficult letter for Halley to compose. As a rejoinder to it he anticipated the worst from Newton. However, when it arrived, it was comparatively mild in tone: 'I thank you for wt you write concerning Mr Hook, for I desire that a good undertaking may be kept between us . . .' Then Newton recommended Halley approach Sir Christopher Wren apropos a conversation between them in 1677. This would clarify for Halley the nature of the Hooke-Newton relationship.

In his Book I, Newton had not mentioned Hooke's name once. The reason, he contended, was that he truly believed he owed nothing contained in this section to him. However, in part of the work Newton had not dispatched to Halley he *had* mentioned him.

On receipt of Newton's mild reply, Halley probably breathed a sigh of relief. Perhaps the worst was over? It was not. It was the calm before the storm. Halley still did not appreciate how Newton's mind worked; how, after a slight, the passage of time seemed only to fuel his indignation. It took Newton three weeks to work up his dander and then commit his true thoughts to paper. Halley now received another letter from Cambridge: 'In order to let you know ye case between Mr Hook & me, I gave you an account of wt past between us in our Letters so far as I could remember . . . I intended in this Letter to let you understand ye case fully but it being a frivilous business, I shal content my self to give you ye heads of it short . . .' Then followed his justification in respect to correspondence he and Hooke had exchanged in earlier years . . .

On the plain face of it there was some justification for an acknowledgement due to Hooke, but Newton was reluctant ever to admit this. Hooke, however, had only *guessed* at the inverse square law whereas Newton had actually demonstrated its mathematical truth. Had Newton possessed a more generous or bending nature, he could have credited Hooke, as a predecessor, as he had credited his other predecessors like Borelli and Wren with part of the ideas he had managed to bring to fruition himself. Indeed, to do so might have enhanced his standing with his supporters in London.

The trouble was, Newton disliked Hooke with an intensity that bordered on a pathological hatred. Earlier in their relationship Hooke had transgressed. It has been Hooke who had reopened correspondence with Newton in 1679 and attempted to re-establish a new relationship between them after Newton's silence following Hooke's criticism of Newton's earlier Theory of Colours. It was now agreed that to avoid any more bad blood they would keep any future disputations strictly to themselves. Soon after, Newton, in replying to Hooke, made a careless blunder over the supposed motion of a body moving towards the Earth's centre. Hooke forgot his promise and gleefully seized the opportunity to broadcast the faux pas at a meeting of the Royal Society, much to Newton's embarrassment. As a result Hooke was never to be trusted again, and it seems Newton was only waiting opportunity for revenge.

Newton told Halley he would not give an inch in his refusal to acknowledge Hooke. He told Halley the second Book was to be a short one, and now only required copying. He explained the third Book, already in draft, would be suppressed for reasons 'Philosophy is such an impertinently litigious Lady that a man had as good be engaged in Law suits as have to do with her. I found so formerly & now I no sooner come near her again but she gives me warning'.

Newton, true to his usual form, composed several versions of this letter before dispatching it to Halley. During successive drafts he received independent information that Hooke was bent on making trouble. In an added postscript to the final draft he went so far as to accuse Hooke of publishing Borelli's ideas under his own name, remarking, sneeringly, that Hooke was incapable of making the calculations to prove them.

In one draft of *Principia*, Newton had started out to acknowledge Hooke's ideas about attraction at distance. Now he vehemently slashed this out of the final version. In his discussion on comets he had also referred to observations made by 'the very distinguished Hooke'. This was first reduced to a more simple 'Hooke' and then at a later date the entire passage was eliminated in order to expunge Hooke's name completely.

Halley, as Newton's editor, friend and confidant, was now in a dilemma. He was faced with an irate author bent on castrating his masterwork. In a rejoinder to Newton he flattered then cajoled him – assuring him that the fellowship at the Society stood firmly behind him. On no account must he suppress Book III. He implored Newton 'not to let your resentments run so high, as to deprive us of your third book, wherein the application of your Mathematicall doctrine to the Theory of Comets, and severall curious Experiments, which, as I guess by what you write, ought to compose it, will undoubtedly render it acceptable to those that will call themselves philosophers without Mathematics, which are by much the greater number'.

In stressing his last point Halley was taking the opportunity to point out it would be unwise to alienate the majority element of the Royal Society fellowship who would find the first two books very hard going. It was a fear later to be realized and then exampled by a wry comment from the President himself – Samuel Pepys.

Halley's letter apparently acted as a balm to Newton's wounded ego. In his reply, Newton even went as far as to admit to Halley his debt to Hooke in three instances. However, he flatly denied Hooke's thinly disguised accusation of plagiarism: with no help from or influence by others he had found the inverse square law as his own original discovery.

Newton agreed not to suppress Book III. Originally, as Halley had indicated in his letter, it was Newton's intention to use this section as an opportunity for a prose essay – a leavening for those representing the majority non-mathematical audience. It was important, as Halley had pointed out, not to make the subject matter too difficult to grasp. As Clerk he knew the limitations of the average Fellow's intellect better than any man. While he agreed not to suppress his third Book, Newton, nevertheless, had a change of heart about its level of erudition. His desire to revenge Hooke's slight clouded his judgement. Newton now informed Halley he would show the 'Smatterer in Mathematics', as he labelled Hooke, what his theories were all about. Sweet revenge for Newton would be to publish *all* the material in a form Hooke would be unable to follow.

Newton's revised Book III contained an important addition to a problem that had finally yielded to his mathematical assault – the comets! Later he admitted. 'This discussion about comets is the most difficult in the whole book.'

Newton, in theory at least, claimed to have solved the age-old problem about the paths of comets. From three evenly spaced observations, measured against the background reference stars whose positions were known with exactitude, the elements of a comet's orbit could be revealed. However, applied to a specific comet the method was still rather hit or miss in its practical application and it depended on placing the middle observation on the orbit by an informed guess. If the guess were not correct, it could be adjusted until the observation fitted. As example he

Above: The return of Halley's comet in 1066 depicted in the famous Bayeux Tapestry.

Below: An old German print showing the famous egg laid in Rome after the appearance of the 1680 comet.

Wunder-Ey.

Welches den ⅓⅔ Decembris dieses mit G.Ott zu Endlauffenden 1680. Heil-Jahrs zu Rom / von einer Henne mit grossen Geschrey ist geleget / und von hoher glaubwürdiger Hand solcher Gestalt in den Entwurff und Abriß gebracht worden.

Above left: Tycho Brahe
(1546-1601).

Above: Charles Messier
(1730-1817).

Left: Isaac Newton (1642-1727).

Above right: The consternation of
London citizens at the
appearance of the great comet of
1811, depicted by the artist
Thomas Rowlandson
(1756-1827).

Right: A comet medallion struck to
commemorate the 1680 comet: 'Th
star threatens evil things. Trust in C
who will turn them to good.'

DER
STERN DROHT
BOESE SACHEN
TRAV· NVR!
GOTT
VVIRDSVVOL
MACHEN·

A° 1680 16 DEC
1681 IAN·

Above: The great comet of 1744, drawn by a contemporary artist, showing its six tails projecting above the horizon.

Left: Giotto's 'Adoration of the Magi' depicting Halley's comet in 1301.

Above right: The great comet of 1843 as seen over Paris. It developed one of the longest tails on record, which, in terms of its true length, was over 220 million kilometres.

Right: A sixpenny pamphlet of 1857 announcing the forthcoming return of the comet of 1264.

Far right: A contemporary impression of Donati's comet in the autumn of 1858 as seen over Paris. The magnificent dust tail appears like a scimitar, and the two narrow gas tails are straight.

WILL THE GREAT COMET now RAPIDLY APPROACHING STRIKE THE EARTH?

LONDON 1857
JAMES GILBERT, 49, PATERNOSTER ROW.
PRICE SIXPENCE.
Or with a Map of the Track of the Comet, Price 8d.

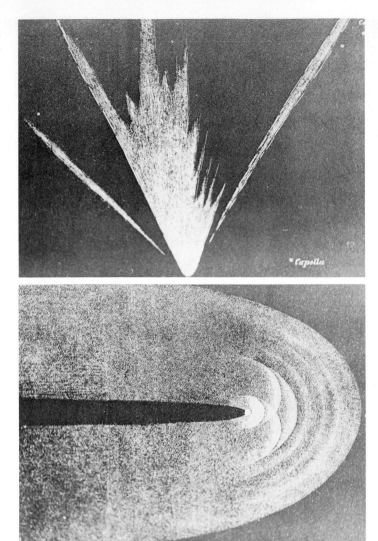

Left: The great comet of 1861 when the Earth passed through its tail on 30 June.

Below left: A contemporary drawing of Coggia's bright comet in July 1874 depicting the expanding envelopes of matter moving out from the nucleus, a phenomenon often seen in bright comets.

Below: The 'Tewfik' Sungrazer comet of 17 May 1882 observed in Egypt during an eclipse of the Sun.

Right: Halley's comet in May 1910 when it shone close to Venus (right). The insets show the tiny, faint images of the comet on 16 and 24 September 1909, a few weeks after its photographic recovery.

Below right: The appearance of Halley's comet on 4 May 1910 as it approached the Earth.

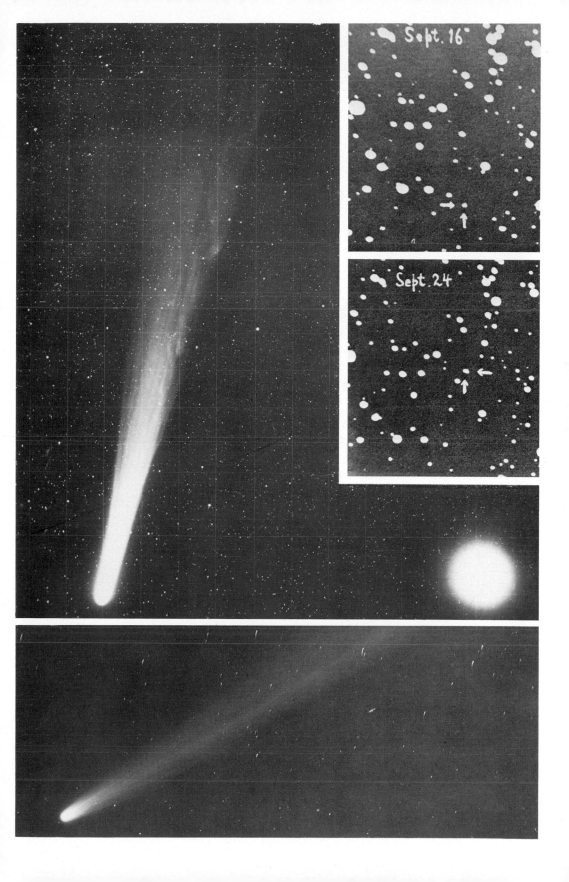

Sungrazing comet Ikeya-Seki (1965 VIII) when it graced the morning skies in early November 1965.

Isaac Newton's detailed notes describing some of his observations of the comet seen in 1682 (later to become known as Halley's comet).

illustrated the path of the 1680-1 comet. By using his trial-and-error (graphical) method he found the comet moved in a plane inclined to the path of the planets (the ecliptic) at an angle tilted at 61° 20 ⅓ ', a figure that agrees fairly well with the more modern calculation of 60°.6779.

Newton's conclusion was the 1680-1 comet travelled round the Sun not in an ellipse like the planets but in a parabola. He was wrong about the choice of conic section, but it was a pretty fair attempt and it provided the groundwork for Halley to develop further some years later. Newton's claim then was that comets are not exceptions to the laws of the solar system and universal gravitation: they obeyed the same dictates of planetary mechanics based on the attraction of the Sun.

Meantime, during the winter of 1686-7 when Newton had finished Book II, publication was suddenly held up by a crisis affecting Halley's own position as Clerk to the Society. It was a direct consequence of his championing of Newton's cause, for he had not reckoned on Hooke's vindictive nature.

Halley's efficiency as Clerk was called into question. On 29 November 1686 the Council were persuaded to take a vote on Halley's continuation in office or whether in his place a new man should be elected.

Although the events leading up to this move are sketchy, we can suppose Hooke to be the ringleader in the conspiracy to oust Halley. In Hooke's eyes Halley was now Newton's accomplice in 'stealing' his ideas for action at distance.

Fortunately for Halley, while neglecting his own astronomical researches to assist Newton, he had been reasonably diligent in the Society's affairs. There must have been some neglect perhaps in the day-to-day correspondence but nothing too serious. Halley so far had been popular as Clerk, and his energy at reorganizing its affairs was commented on favourably. Since his appointment he had not allowed the Clerkship to become a dogsbody post and had elevated the office to something on a par with that of the Honorary Secretaries whose burdensome work he had been appointed to relieve. After taking up the Clerkship he had injected purpose into the weekly meetings, and the *Philosophical Transactions*, the official publication of the Society which before his appointment had been allowed to lapse, was started again.

Significantly, Hooke had been elected to Council that year, and his voice as a long-standing Fellow and one of the Society's founder members carried influence. He was a significant force to be reckoned with. During the winter months of 1686-7 there was lobbying by Hooke's cronies to oust the popular young Clerk. It seems too that Hooke had become jealous of Halley's success in the Clerkship. Before Halley's time, Hooke, as Curator of Experiments, was responsible for 'entertaining' the fellows at the weekly meetings. Although very able and a scientist of the first magnitude, his personality and overbearing attitude to others worked against his popularity. He made enemies at the drop of a hat, and his reputation for irascibility and crotchetiness was well known to everybody.

On 5 January 1687, a committee was formed to investigate Halley's alleged misconduct and at the same time it invited Hooke to bring in a proposal to supply meetings – for a salary – 'with experiments & discourse'.

Halley's friends rallied to help him. In a letter to Newton dated February 1687 explaining circumstances in London, he reported that '6 of 38, last generall Election day, did endeavour to have me put by'. Halley maintained a brave front through the episode while his fate hung in the balance; he refused to involve himself in vindictive counterploys. This detachment did much to impress the neutral members of the committee. When it met again to report in his favour, he wrote to Newton the following day, enthusiastic about plans for pushing ahead again with the publication of *Principia*.

It was Halley too who spared Newton much of the drudgery in providing the printers with a fair working copy. He told a friend 'the corrections of the press costs me a great deal of time & paines'. As a reward Halley received a handsome acknowledgement from Newton in the preface. In later years Newton often referred to *Principia* as 'Halley's book'.

As the text was extremely complicated, there were constant delays due to repeated corrections to printers' errors, but at last, on 5 July 1687, Halley was able to tell Newton 'I have at length brought your Book to an end, and hope it will please you . . . I have sent you to bestow on your friends in the University 20 Copies, which I entreat you to accept'.

The finished work was a 500-page masterpiece containing 97 propositions in the first book, 53 in the second and 42 in the third. It was priced at nine shillings, in small quarto, and printed in Latin as had become custom. The title page read *Philosophiae naturalis principia mathematica* (the *Mathematical Principles of Natural Philosophy*) and was given the imprimatur of Samuel Pepys as President of the Royal Society.

The pith of the book was Newton's now famous three laws:

1. A body remains at rest or continues to move in the same straight line with constant speed unless it is acted upon by another force.
2. The force applied to a body is in the direction of the acceleration

imparted to the body, and is equal to the mass of the body times its acceleration.
3. Every action has an equal and opposite reaction.

Principia still remains one of the greatest, if not *the* greatest, scientific book ever written. So what did Pepys himself make of it in 1687? Not much, it seems. Pepys, by his own admission, was never any kind of scientist. The only scientific book that had impressed him was Hooke's 'ingenious' *Micrographia*, and then it was really only the plates in the book which attracted him. All other scientific books gave him difficulty. If truth be known, he did not understand even what Newton was writing about! In a letter dated August 1688 to his old tutor Joseph Hill, Pepys refers wryly to two prevailing mysteries: one being 'Mr Newton's *Principia* which is understood by few but deservedly admired by all those who understand it' and the second 'the activity of the Dutch fleet' whose purport, at least to Pepys, seemed far more intelligent to the lay mind.

But Sam Pepys was not the only one baffled by *Principia*. Newton presented a copy to one of his colleagues at Trinity, Dr Babington, who reported after having perused its contents 'he might study it seven years before he understood anything of it'. Few, if any, of Newton's colleagues at Cambridge could make much more of it either. When Newton passed a student and his companion in a Cambridge street just after publication, the student is purported to have remarked: 'There goes the man that writt a book that neither he nor any body else understands.'

Its word-of-mouth reputation, however, as being 'the key to the mysteries of the universe' was soon awesome. Booksellers were inundated by a very curious lay public who wished to buy 'a translation' of it, and it seems that a rendering into the English language from its original Latin was not the only object its potential readership had in mind. Although Newton's book was translated into English by Andrew Motte in 1729, it wasn't until James Ferguson (1710-76), a poor Scottish farm labourer who became an astronomer, wrote his bestselling *Astronomy explained upon Sir Isaac Newton's Principles* (1756) that Newton's ideas were much understood by the intelligent lay public. Ferguson's book was so eagerly devoured that during his lifetime it went through six editions.

Success for Newton after the publication of *Principia* in 1687 was heralded by the decline of Hooke as a man of influence. Unfortunately suffering from a disfigurement of his spine since birth and outwardly unattractive, Hooke's unlikeable personality had gradually lost him friends. Nevertheless, he was a man of considerable intellect; had he been born in another age, he might have been better remembered as one of England's greatest scientists. As it was, Newton overshadowed him as he also overshadowed Halley. Even so, Hooke was to have his champions right into the twentieth century. Like Newton, he remained a bachelor, but, unlike Newton who was a latent homosexual, he conducted torrid affairs with successive housekeepers at Gresham College where he was Professor of Geometry. Like his contemporary Sam Pepys, he entered details of his dalliances in a diary, recording them cryptically. When his favourite niece, the daughter of a brother who had committed suicide, replaced a housekeeper, he fell victim to the grand passion of his life. Now middle-aged he doted on her, but she drove him to distraction by her unfaithfulness. She died the same year *Principia* was published so the year 1687 was a particularly black one for him.

4 · 'A Synopsis of Comets'

FTER THE LABOURS of seeing *Principia* through the press, Halley reimmersed himself in the routine business of the Royal Society and his own scientific work. In the following year he published three papers, one of which would have influence in determining the course of his life and involve him in controversy. It was a theme treated earlier by Hooke and others – namely the cause of the biblical flood, a subject which held a universal fascination in Halley's day. One idea was that the flood had been due to a shift of the Earth's poles, and in restating this idea Halley concluded the flood must have occurred in the very distant past. He was treading on dangerous ground, for the inference was that the time-scale then accepted by churchmen for the creation of the world was in error.

Halley did not openly dispute the date of '9 am 23 October 4004 BC', then held to be the exact time for the Creation, but to even hint it might be in error was tantamount to the crime of heresy – a serious, damaging charge in a society where the establishment was dominated by influential bishops. Dabblers in Church chronology could soon find themselves having to answer to authority.

Halley suggested the flood may have been caused by the Earth's close encounter with a comet or some other wandering cosmic body. He argued that both pagan as well as biblical sources indicated the deluge occurred as a sudden catastrophic event. An approaching comet, therefore, would

63

aptly supply the mechanism to trigger a gravitational upheaval. Although Newton's work had shown that comets were subject to the laws of universal gravitation, it had shed no light on the physical nature of comets. The mass of a typical comet remained unknown, but contemporary opinion believed them to be substantial bodies akin to the planets; such a body, reasoned Halley, might change the length of the year and the shape (eccentricity) of the Earth's orbit. Unwittingly, Halley's paper opened the floodgates for countless similar theories put forward since his time involving the possible catastrophic influences of wandering comets on the Earth. Most of these even today are based on the faulty assumption that comets have substantial mass.

But Halley's interests were wide ranging, and comets were only one facet of his researches. In the late 1680s and early '90s he was formulating and experimenting on a variety of problems spanning new ideas in astronomy, Earth sciences, chronology and nautical matters. Since his voyage to St Helena he had retained a great interest in the sea. He seems to have read many of the books about English and Dutch voyages which at this time, before the popularity of fiction, were the bestsellers of their age. These narratives tended to make him restless. We know he had no wish to remain as the paid Clerk to the Society for the rest of his working life and he was constantly casting his eye round for a position that would lead to intellectual and social betterment and provide more time for his own scientific researches.

In the early 1690s, while still Clerk, he was away at Pagham in Sussex working on a prototype diving-bell, using a frigate loaned by the Admiralty for the purpose. Diving and diving-bells were recognized to have great potential use, and the Admiralty seems to have looked upon the young astronomer's new expertise with favour. It was in June 1691, while still at Pagham, he heard news that his old Oxford professor Edward Bernard had resigned the Savilian Chair of Astronomy. Without delay he put forward his name for the vacancy, realizing that he stood an excellent chance of the appointment. However, the new professor had to be approved by the Church, and soon disquieting news reached him making him aware that prominent churchmen had not forgotten the young astronomer who had 'tampered with chronology'.

In a letter from Pagham to his influential friend and colleague Abraham Hill (1635-1722), Halley wrote: '. . . an affair of great consequence to myself calls me to London, viz Looking after the Astronomy-Professor's place in Oxford, I humbly beg of you to intercede for me with the arch:bishop Dr Tillotson, to defer the election for some short time, 'till I have done here if it be but for a fortnight: but it must be done with expedition, lest it be too late to speak. This time will give me an opportunity tó clear myself in another matter . . . there being a caveat entered against me, till I can show that I am not guilty of asserting the eternity of the world.'

The chickens had come home to roost! Halley must have felt a little like Bruno or Galileo before the Inquisition.

Other candidates with reputations were also vying for the professorship. One of the front runners was David Gregory (1661-1708), a new acolyte of Newton. Earlier, Gregory, a professor of mathematics at Edinburgh, had sought to establish a close friendship with Newton by correspondence. From the start his motives were self-interest, and he courted Newton's favour in a shameless manner. Then, when the astronomy professorship vacancy was declared, his long siege of Newton's patronage was rewarded, and Newton agreed he would support his application.

The question is: why did Newton support Gregory rather than his old friend Halley – the man he owed more to than any other? Perhaps he thought Gregory was a better candidate? Doubtful. Newton well knew that Halley's intellect was one that closely matched his own and perhaps in some common spheres of interest surpassed his own. Was Newton's support of Gregory then to keep Halley in his place as Clerk to the Society to prevent him gaining a professorship and becoming a rival to fame? Again doubtful. Was it due to Halley's incursion into Church affairs with his too public a hint about the errors in Church chronology? Very likely. By now Newton was strongly religious, but his own commitment to Arianism was not something he broadcast. According to Thomas Hearne, Halley's frequent irreverence in respect to religious matters often upset Newton. By backing Gregory's application it seems that Newton avoided the embarrassment of supporting a more controversial candidate – yet one wonders how much heart-searching this cost him.

One of the Church's referees for the appointment was Bishop Stillingfleet (1635-99) then bishop of Worcester. According to Hearne's account, the bishop, during the interview with Halley, taxed him with some religious questions. Halley is reputed to have replied: 'My Lord, that is not the business I came about. I declare myself a Christian and hope to be treated as such.'

However, according to William Whiston (1667-1752), later to occupy Newton's Lucasian Chair in Mathematics at Cambridge, the bishop went as far as to request Halley to recant his disbeliefs expressed when he wrote his paper about the deluge, but Halley refused to do so on principle.

Whatever the truth of these stories, Halley arrived to meet the bishop armed with the knowledge that his old Oxford college was fully behind his candidature: 'We judge him to be in every way most fit and accomplished for this performance as well as from our own long experience of his mathematical genius, probity, sobriety, and good life as from the very many testimonials of all foreigners.'

The Council of the Royal Society also gave him a strong recommendation.

Before the interview it is likely that the bishop's chaplain, Richard Bentley, was asked to investigate the nature of Halley's alleged heresies so as to have the facts readily to hand. Bentley (1662-1742) is a curious character in the story of Halley and Newton. From a distance he had long been an admirer of Newton. After ingratiating himself into Newton's favour, he was in later years to edit *Principia* for a second edition and made a point of not consulting Halley at all over changes in the text and even tampered with some glowing Latin hexameters composed by Halley in praise of Newton which he had included in the first edition. Halley was not the only author to suffer at the hands of Bentley; he even made amendments in an edition of Milton's *Paradise Lost*.

It is surprising that Halley did not ask his old school chum and grand-tour companion Robert Nelson to intercede with a good opinion to the bishops. If he did, it is not recorded. By now Nelson, a highly religious man, had much influence with the senior bishops – especially John Tillotson, Archbishop of Canterbury – but whether, as with Newton, Halley's supposed heresies proved an embarrassment is unknown.

Whatever occurred at the bishop's interview, Halley was not appointed to the vacancy. This went to Newton's choice of candidate, Gregory. Stemming from this is a wry anecdote, which circulated in the London coffee-houses shortly after, about a certain Scotsman who, on hearing of the bishop's preference over Halley, travelled immediately to London to meet a man with less religion than Gregory.

It seems that Flamsteed also played a part in spoking Halley's aspirations for the professorship. The pious Flamsteed was by now openly at loggerheads with Halley. There are several stories which relate to the supposed reason for the breach with Flamsteed, but the truth of the cause is another of the uncertainties dogging the details of Halley's life. One story relates that the usually diplomatic Halley dropped an unfortunate remark, albeit an innocent one, about some corrections he thought necessary to some tidal tables drawn up by the tetchy Flamsteed who, ever jealous of his reputation, took affront and accused Halley of slighting his character. Nevertheless, there are other equally cogent explanations for their quarrel (*see p. 31*). Whatever the cause of the alleged offence Halley had committed, Flamsteed was so angered that when he heard the Oxford professorship was vacant and Halley was a candidate, he wrote to exhort Newton to prevent his election for the reason that he would 'corrupt ye youth of ye University with his lewd discourse'.

Even so, it is doubtful if this was the key influencing factor that persuaded Newton to back Gregory rather than Halley. A few years later Newton himself was to be involved in a contretemps with the Astronomer Royal.

Whether Bishop Stillingfleet had heard whispers of Halley's alleged exploits in St Helena and in Danzig − or in other circumstances now unknown to us − is a matter for conjecture. The accusations of past heresies on Halley's part might well have provided a convenient reason for the bishop to debar Halley from a university appointment. Re-reading Halley's papers about comets and the deluge, three hundred years on, it is difficult to see on what evidence he was accused of heresy − even taking into account the sensitive feelings of churchmen at that time.

So what were Halley's religious views? In truth he was a deist: he believed God existed and created the world but thereafter assumed no control over it or the lives of people.[1]

Halley apparently took his setback to an academic career in his stride. If university life was debarred him, there was still the sea! Many of his scientific papers round this time concern subjects with a strong nautical flavour. For example: 'An Instrument for Measuring the Way of a Ship'; and 'A Method of Enabling a Ship to carry its Guns in Bad Weather'. There was also a paper for the design of a quadrant with telescopic sights.

Another problem which fascinated him was the rate of evaporation of sea-water. Could this, he wondered, provide a significant clue to the puzzle of the age of the oceans and hence in turn the true age of the Earth? He was still an unreformed 'dabbler in chronology'. He argued if the oceans had begun as fresh water, their increasing salinity, year by year, century by century, was a direct measure of time. He concluded from this study a great age for the Earth, far in excess of estimates by churchmen based on the Book of Genesis.

In 1693, Halley and a friend called Benjamin Middleton began to plan a scientific voyage about which little is known except for its brief mention in Hooke's diary and some Royal Society and Admiralty documents. The short of it was, according to Hooke's diary, 'Halley & Middleton made proposalls of going into ye South Sea & Round the World'.

67

Apparently Halley and his friend approached the Royal Society for assistance to secure '. . . a small vessel of 60 Tuns . . . in order to encompass the Globe to make observations on the Magneticall Needle, & c'.

We know the Navy Board were favourably disposed towards the idea. Its members were already impressed with Halley's work on diving-bells and his apparent familiarity, for a man of science, with practical naval problems. In 1694 a vessel, a new Pink, called the *Paramore* (sometimes spelt *Paramour* or *Parrimore*) was constructed for the requirements of the proposed voyage, and at the same time Halley, still holding office as the Royal Society's Clerk, received a royal commission appointing him master and commander. With the appointment came an authorization to equip the vessel with a regular complement of naval officers and crew. It now seemed certain that Halley was about to launch himself in a new career as a scientific voyager. The reason why he delayed was probably due to some disagreement with the Admiralty over expenses for provisioning and crew wages which initially were to be provided by Halley's backers. Owing to this delay, Halley cast his mind to other matters.

*   *   *

In 1695, Newton and Halley entered into a vigorous correspondence about comets. For eight years, since the publication of *Principia* there had only been occasional social contacts between them. We know that in the interim Halley had entertained Newton several times at his London home; if he had held any resentments over the preferment for Gregory, we read nothing about it.

In *Principia* Newton had argued that the path of the 1680-1 comet was in the shape of a parabola. After dismissing the idea of a rectilinear orbit, there had been a choice of three possible curves: a closed one like that described by the planets – the ellipse; the open-ended parabola; or the hyperbola. Newton had in turn rejected the closed ellipse (which he would have preferred) and the hyperbola; this was in spite of earlier ideas shared by Hooke, Seth Ward and others that ellipses probably suited the paths of comets best. However, using his choice of parabola, Newton made the break-through. By providing a method and formal proof he showed that a parabolic path most suited all the observations made of the 1680-1 comet.

By 1695, Halley had advanced in his own researches into the paths of comets. Accepting nothing on trust, he worked through historical records to glean any information about comets which had appeared in the past. He was searching for data in the form of observations he could use to calculate orbits, using the now established Newtonian principles of universal gravitation. He even rechecked Newton's work.

Periodically he gave progress reports to Newton. In one letter he writes: '. . . I fell to consider that [comet] of 1680-1 which you have described in your book [*Principia*], and looking over your catalogue of observed places, I find in that of the 25th January 1681, there is a mistake of 20 minutes in the celestial Longitude of that day, or 56 minutes for 36, and so I have it in a lre [letter] Mr Flamsteed sent me when I was in Paris. I thought fitt to advertise this, because you wrote you designed to undertake to correct what you had formerly determined about the Orb thereof; and that day is one of those you have taken to define the orb by . . .'

Newton must have been annoyed to read about this careless error committed to print in his masterwork. It may also have rankled when he learned from Halley 'I find certain indications of an Elliptick orb in that Comet and am satisfied that it will be very difficult to hitt it exactly by a Parabolick. When I have computed all the Observations, I shall send you what I have done'.

Halley believed he was on the threshold of another breakthrough in cometary astronomy. Newton had provided the apparatus, but ironically the very example he had used to illustrate its working method was defective. As the leading disciple of Newton, and his ex-editor, Halley understood *Principia* better than any other man. In addition, his flair for historical scholarship was superior to that of Newton's; his comet researches were turning up useful observations of past comets stretching back to times before Tycho Brahe and Kepler.

Past observations were the key to Halley's new researches. He knew that Flamsteed had made some excellent observations of the 1682 comet, the comet he himself had observed from Islington shortly after his marriage. The problem now was how he was going to prise them loose from the man who wished to discredit him at every opportunity. His standing with Flamsteed was at a particularly low point. On 7 February 1695 the Astronomer Royal had written to Newton: 'I have done with him [Halley] who has almost ruined himselfe by his indiscreet behaviour. & you shall hear no more of him from me . . . till wee meet when I shall tell you his history which is too foule and large for a letter.'

These 'too foule and large' deeds do not seem to have prejudiced Newton's opinion of Halley. In desiring Flamsteed's observations of the

1682 comet, Halley took the obvious way out and requested Newton to solicit them from the Astronomer Royal. Newton owed Halley a favour. Significantly Halley wrote to Cambridge: 'I must entreat you to procure for me of Mr Flamsteed what he has observed of the Comett of 1682 particularly in the month of September, for I am more confirmed that we have seen that Comett now three times, since ye yeare 1531, he will not deny it you though I know he will me.'

Halley had indeed made the break-through but was not yet sure of all his facts; on the face of it the 1682 comet had been a returning periodic comet seen on two previous occasions – possibly three.

Newton obtained the necessary observations. Halley, on receipt of them, recognized their true worth and gave generous praise to the man who had made them. He replied to Newton, expressing his wish that Flamsteed had made similar high-quality observations for the 1680-1 comet as all the other observations Halley had collated were from 'very course observers'.

Halley's plan when he began his new comet researches was to extend the scope of Newton's earlier work. In applying universal gravitation to comets he wondered about the consequences of the effect large planets might have on comets. Seeking guidance, he wrote to Newton: 'I must entreat you to consider how far a Comet's motion may be disturbed by the Centres of Saturn & Jupiter particular in its ascent [its retreating path] from the Sun and what difference they may cause in the time of the Revolution of a Comet in its so very Elliptick Orb.'

Halley had put his finger on the key to the calculation of cometary orbits. He had recognized that in the case of comets moving in very eccentric orbits those passing close to massive bodies like Jupiter and Saturn might be subject to unusual gravitational pulls.

Halley included in his study the Plague and the Fire comets he had seen from the City as a boy. The 1664 Plague comet gave him his greatest problem. In attempts to calculate its orbit he tried using observations of his old acquaintance Hevelius, now dead for some eight years. He soon suspected the wily Danzig astronomer had cooked his observations by adding '8 or 9 minutes to make his figures agree' to the places observed.

Halley's aim was not simply to rationalize observations made in the past to obtain orbits; he was looking for comets whose future paths could be predicted as astronomers could predict the paths of the planets. To do this he needed to know whether Jupiter and Saturn would hold a comet back in its course or alternatively accelerate it.

The two comets that interested him most were the 1680-1 comet and the 1682 comet which he already suspected had been seen previously. In the case of the 1680-1 comet he finally discarded Newton's notion of a parabolic orbit and substituted an elliptical one that gave the comet a revolution period round the Sun of 575 years. Such a comet would journey into space far beyond the distance of Saturn. Thus Halley realized the Sun's influence and the solar system itself must be much greater than astronomers at the time supposed.

However, the results he had obtained for the 1682 comet were even more interesting. If his calculations for the 1680-1 comet were correct, this comet would not be seen again until the year 2255, whereas the results for the 1682 comet indicated a revolution period round the Sun of about 75/76 years!

In arriving at this period for the 1682 comet, he was guided by knowledge that Kepler (and Longomontanus [1562-1647], who had also been assistant to Tycho Brahe) had observed a bright comet in 1607 and previous to that one had been seen by Peter Apian in 1531. Yet another comet had been seen in 1456. The computed elements of their respective orbits – their orbital 'fingerprints' – looked remarkably similar. For this reason he felt justified in discounting coincidence.

Even now, however, Halley held back from making public his findings. His comet researches were interrupted by outside events. It was to be several years before he finally published his intriguing prediction. Halley had already delayed his scientific voyage to the South Seas; and when Newton suddenly offered him an appointment, his career took off at an entirely new tangent.

The Parliament of the day had become very concerned over the widespread practice of coin clipping, and the nation's whole economy was threatened by it. Only coins impressed with a distinct milled edge were safe. When the government decided to recoin, Newton and other influential figures of the day were asked to advise on how this should be done.

It was a turning-point in Newton's life. He was appointed Warden of the Mint. He deserted Cambridge and entered London life as a public servant and he was soon to become a very successful bureaucrat. Just before this he had reached a low point in his life and for a time in 1693 was victim to a total nervous breakdown but he recovered quickly. As Warden of the Mint his latent administrative powers were given opportunity for fulfilment. Few had appreciated that the Cambridge recluse – author of the very abtruse *Principia* – was a man of great organizational ability. From here on Newton's days as a scientific researcher were over.

His task was to organize regional mints in Norwich, York, Bristol, Exeter and Chester. He quickly realized he needed men of integrity to supervise the work of these outpost mints. It was now that he contacted Halley who by late 1696 was ensconced as Deputy Comtroller at Chester at a salary of £90 per annum.

While Newton thrived in his new position directing affairs in London, Halley was less successful in Chester. He was unhappy to be involved in the day-to-day squabblings of petty officialdom and although he performed his duties diligently, he found himself having to defend his actions. In the end Newton's assistance was called upon to protect his appointee's honour. He defended Halley brilliantly before the Lords' Commissioners and carried the day. Grateful for Newton's patronage and help, Halley remained in Chester until the country mints were closed in 1698.

If Chester proved one thing for Halley, it was he had no talent for commerce. He was still officially Clerk to the Society, but soon the long-postponed scientific voyage was in the air again. On 15 October 1698 the Admiralty renewed their interest and on Halley's own recommendation issued instructions for a twelve months' scientific voyage designed to investigate and improve knowledge about magnetic variations. By this time, however, his friend Middleton had disappeared from the scene, and we hear no more of him.

As the expedition commander, Halley was directed: '. . . to make the best of your way to the Southward of the Equator and there observe on the East Coast of South America, and the West Coast of Africa the variations of the Compasse, with all the accuracy you can . . . you are likewise to make like observations at as many of the Islands in the Seas between the aforesaid coasts as you can . . . and if the season of the Yeare permit, you are to stand soe farr into the South, Till you discover the Coast of Terra Incognita.'

Before Halley sailed for the South Seas on what was to be the first of three voyages, Czar Peter (1672-1725) arrived in London to study English shipbuilding. He was a guest of the government, and it was arranged he should reside with his entourage in Evelyn's house at Deptford, conveniently adjacent to the Thames shipyards.

It is supposed that Peter asked to be put in touch with the most knowledgeable Englishmen and, according to some sources, Halley was one of those selected.

Peter's reputation is legendary. Studying English shipbuilding for him meant the day-to-day toil of working as a shipwright himself, and contemporary accounts tell of his fondness for showing off the rough calluses on his hands. He was seized with a great zest for life. Very tall, his temperament was mercurial and, according to several ladies from the courts of Europe, 'exceedingly vulgar'. Nevertheless, he was highly intelligent and a man with an insatiable appetite for knowledge as well as for the corporeal pleasures of the flesh. It is said Peter introduced the habit of drinking brandy into England, and it is of interest that Flamsteed in later years was to accuse Halley of indulging in this new fashion.

When he arrived in London, Peter was still only twenty-six years old. By now Halley was forty-two. It is recounted that Peter immediately took to Halley and 'admitted him to the familiarity of his table'. Peter's education had only been perfunctory. He spoke no English and apart from his native Russian possessed only an elementary smattering of Dutch and German. If Halley and Peter did talk tête-à-tête, it was likely to have been in Dutch or German. Halley was good at languages, although little is known of how well he spoke them. He had studied German for his stay in Danzig and later he used German during his missions abroad for Queen Anne in the period immediately following his voyages. He read Dutch reasonably well, and one of his principal reference sources for his comet researches was a book in High Dutch.

Nevertheless, little is known about Halley's brief relationship with the Czar. In most contemporary accounts of the Czar's stay in London, Halley's name is not mentioned; the fact that he met the Czar, and dined at his table, is based on the hearsay of Halley's near contemporaries.

In truth, the meeting between Halley and the Czar likely came about due to Peter's interest in the *Paramore* – the vessel the Admiralty had put at Halley's disposal for his long-postponed scientific voyage. She was 64 feet long with a tonnage of 89 and she attracted Peter's attention. We know he made a request that she be rigged and made seaworthy so he could carry out sailing experiments with her. Peter was so much impressed with the Royal Navy he is alleged to have remarked: 'I would rather be an admiral in England than a Czar in Russia.'

Peter's stay at Deptford created a scandal. His hard drinking and horseplay round the house and garden was the talk of London. Evelyn's delightful home was turned into a shambles. It seems, however, several of the stories about the Czar's antics were much exaggerated. Whether Halley was a participant in Peter's wild drinking-sprees is unknown; in view of Flamsteed's later remarks about Halley's alleged new fondness for brandy one might speculate that it was the Czar who possibly introduced it to him.

Halley sailed from Deptford on his first scientific voyage on 20 October 1698. The new commander of His Majesty's Pink *Paramore* was soon to be involved with the trouble of a disobedient crew. Because of his lack of deep-sea experience in command of a vessel, we can assume that most of the regular officers of the navy seconded for the voyage would be a little resentful of the gentleman amateur placed in charge. Halley's only experience of a long voyage was the one he had made as a passenger to St Helena twenty-odd years previously. He had worked on naval vessels during his experiments with diving-bells, but these were conducted among inshore sheltered waters. Such a man might easily make himself a laughing-stock to those who served under him on a voyage to the South Seas.

Apparently, however, there was more to the discontentment than the commander's lack of experience. In spite of this, Halley soon got the hang of things. His chief problem stemmed from his first lieutenant, a man called Harrison. Whatever the merits of the new commander, Harrison was bent on making trouble from the outset of the voyage and tried to undermine the rest of the crew's confidence in him. The first lieutenant held a grudge against Halley and it seems probable he had purposely secured his appointment to the *Paramore* with the aim of showing Halley's capabilities in poor light. In 1696, Harrison had published a small volume in which he had proposed a method of determining accurate longitude at sea. This was submitted to the Admiralty who, in its wisdom, appointed a panel of experts to adjudicate on it. One of the experts was Halley.

The finding of the panel was that Harrison's ideas were incompetent as well as impractical. Harrison had been unable to forget or forgive this slight, and we can surmise it was with malice aforethought that he volunteered for duty with Halley's expedition.

The upshot of Harrison's open disobedience was that Halley decided to abandon his first voyage. He turned his ship round and navigated it across the stormy Atlantic back to England without any help. He reached Plymouth on 23 June 1699. In due course Harrison faced a court-martial, and it was left to the Lords of the Admiralty to decide his fate.

After his return Halley readily admitted his own lack of experience: 'perhaps I have not the whole Sea Dictionary so perfect as he . . . he for a long time made it his business to represent me, to the whole Shipps company, as a person wholly unqualified for the command their [Lordships] have given me, and declaring that he was sent on board here, because their Lordships knew my insufficiency.'

Harrison survived his court-martial with only a stern reprimand – a light sentence for a crime bordering on mutiny. Technically he was able to prove he had not actually disobeyed Halley's orders; the only charge to stick was one of insolence. Had he been court-martialled a hundred years later when conditions were much harsher in the British navy, he could have faced possible death even for this minor offence. As it was, the court-martial's regular officers were sympathetic to Harrison and let him off lightly. Fortunately the Admiralty recognized the incident in its true light and retained faith in Halley who was already making preparations for a second voyage.

He sailed again on 27 September 1699 and by 27 January the following year was pushing south towards the unknown Terra Incognita. Halley never reached the shores of the Antarctic continent, having been repulsed by huge and dangerous tabular icebergs blocking his route. During his voyage he carried out intensive magnetic observations and arrived back in England in August 1700.

Even now his voyaging days were not over, and on 14 June 1701 he sailed from Deptford again, this time on a secret mission for the Admiralty to reconnoitre the French Channel ports under the pretext of another scientific voyage. When he returned to Deptford on 10 October 1701, his brief but adventurous naval career was over.

Affairs in Europe at this time were tense. In September 1701, Leopold of Austria entered into the Grand Alliance with the English and the Dutch. When Queen Anne ascended the throne in 1702, it was decided to send Halley abroad to Vienna as her special emissary to advise the Emperor on the fortifications of the harbours along the northern shores of the Adriatic.

Halley made two journeys to Europe, the second was to supervise the works he had recommended during his first visit. He received a valuable gold ring from the Emperor for services rendered. Little is known about the semi-clandestine mission in the Channel or his two missions on behalf of Queen Anne. Contemporary state records shed very little light on the toing and froing of 'Captain Halley's' covert operations except for the significant fact his expense monies in Vienna were funded 'out of the secret service'.

Halley's next change of course was signalled in October 1703, a month before he returned to London from the Continent. In Oxford the Rev. John Wallis, Savilian Professor of Geometry, died, and a vacancy was declared. Friends of Halley immediately put forward his name. His old adversary Bishop Stillingfleet had been dead for four years and was no threat. Bentley, the bishop's ex-chaplain and fellow conspirator to keep

'the infidel mathematician' – as Bentley called him – from the
astronomy professorship in 1691, was by now far too busy, immersed in
his own self-made troubles as Master of Trinity at Cambridge to bother
about Halley. Nevertheless, Flamsteed was still prepared to put down his
ex-protégé whenever the opportunity was offered him. In December 1703
he wrote to his ex-assistant Abraham Sharpe: 'Dr Wallis is dead. Mr
Halley expects his place. He now talks, swears, and drinks brandy like a
sea captain, so that I much fear his own ill-behaviour will deprive him of
the vacancy.'

Halley, however, was riding on the crest of his newly won reputation.
As a scientific voyager he had enjoyed a great success, and his semi-covert
missions to Vienna on behalf of the government had enhanced his status.
He was on good terms with Newton who, as Master of the Mint and
President-elect of the Royal Society, was one of the most influential men
in England.

On 30 November 1703, Halley was elected to the Council of the Royal
Society, actually gaining more votes in the ballot than Newton.
Flamsteed's vindictiveness could not stop him; with very little opposition
Halley was duly elected to fill the Savilian Chair of Geometry at Oxford.
In May 1704 he returned to his Alma Mater to deliver his inaugural
lecture.

He was now forty-eight years old. He had at last secured a sheltered
cloister where he could pursue his scientific work. Round the University
he was known and addressed as 'Captain Halley' and as an academic he
must have been rather proud of this unique distinction. It was not until he
received an honorary degree from Oxford in 1710 that people switched to
calling him Dr Halley.

One piece of work he was anxious to finalize was his researches into
comets. Much of the groundwork and drudgery of calculation had been
done before he went to the Chester Mint in 1696. Now he revised what he
had done previously and prepared it for the press. In 1705 he published it
under the title *Astronomie Cometicae Synopsis* and simultaneously in English
as *A Synopsis of the Astronomy of Comets*. It was also reprinted in *Philosophical
Transactions*.

As the title suggests, it is a short book. In sharp contrast to Newton's
500-odd-page *Principia*, Halley's tract was only double the length of
Newton's original *De motu*. The historical introduction is accomplished in
three pages, and the kernel (the Synopsis) of the whole work is contained
in a table giving the (parabolic) elements of twenty-four comets *(see p.
179)*.

To derive these orbits in a pre-computer age had involved Halley in a task of the most gruelling tedium. Twenty years before, Newton had provided the methods and insights; now by heroic application Halley as the leading practitioner of Newtonianism reaped the harvest of the comets which had eluded Newton himself.

As Halley summed up: '. . . Hitherto I have considered the Orbits of comets as exactly Parabolick; upon which Supposition it wou'd follow that Comets being impell'd towards the Sun by a Centripetal Force descend as from Spaces infinitely distant, and by their Falls acquire such a Velocity, as they may again run off into the remotest Parts of the Universe, moving upwards with such a perpetual Tendency, as never to return again to the Sun. But since they appear frequently enough, and since none of them can be found to move with a Hyperbolick Motion, or a Motion swifter than what a Comet might acquire by its gravity to the Sun, 'tis highly probable that they rather move in very Excentric Orbits, and make their Returns after long Periods of Time: For so their Number will be determinate, and perhaps, not so very great.

'. . . And indeed, there are many Things which make me believe that the Comet which Apian [Peter Apian (1495-1552)] observed in the year 1531 was the same with that which *Kepler* and Longomontanus took notice of and describ'd in the Year 1607, and which I myself have seen return, & observ'd in the Year 1682. All the Elements [orbital details] agree, and nothing seems to contradict this my Opinion, besides the Inequality of the Periodick Revolutions: Which Inequality is not so great neither, as that it may not be owing to Physical Causes. For the motion of Saturn is so disturbed by the rest of the Planets, especially *Jupiter*, that the Periodick

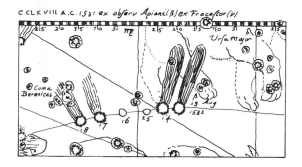

Fig. 7   The path of Halley's comet in 1531 as plotted by Peter Apian in Ingolstadt and Fracastor in Verona (taken from Theatrum Cometicum). *This was the first of three apparitions used by Halley.*

Time of the Planet is uncertain for some whole Days together. How much more therefore will a Comet be subject to such Errors, which rises almost Four times, higher than Saturn and whose velocity, tho' encreased but very little would be sufficient to change its Orbit, from an Elliptical to a Parabolical one, . . .'

Halley's principal message then was that the great comet seen in 1682 was moving in an elliptical path only a little inclined to that of the major planets and that its period of revolution round the Sun would bring it back near the Earth and Sun some time in the year 1758.

In 1705 this event was over half a century into the future. Halley was forty-nine years old. The chances were he would be dead and so would most of his contemporaries. Such a prediction was interesting, but it was too far ahead to occupy much interest. Neither could the claim yet be proven.

Newton was very impressed with the thoroughness of Halley's work. In the revision of the *Principia* he included additional material about comets with special reference to the 1680-1 comet to which in his *Synopsis* Halley had assigned a period of 575 years.

In arriving at 575 years for the 1680-1 comet, Halley based his calculations on the same observations which had been available to Newton. While Halley was more astute than Newton in realizing all comets were periodic, i.e. revolved round the Sun in ellipses, he was never to realize how eccentric (near parabolic) some of these ellipses could be. In 1818 the German astronomer Johann Franz Encke, using newer methods, found it was difficult to pinpoint the orbital period of the 1680-1 comet with any accuracy owing to slight discrepancies in the observations made by Newton and Halley and their contemporaries. In fact, using all the available observations, the period of the comet could be alternatively 805 years; 3,164 years; 8,800 years or possibly the comet might have a hyperbolic path. The latter would imply that after passing round the Sun and moving off into space the comet would never return to the solar system. Such comets with hyperbolic paths have been recognized in modern times, but these characteristics were impressed on them *after* they entered the domain of the Sun.

*   *   *

Following the publication of *Synopsis*, Halley settled down at Oxford to compose a long series of scientific papers. His work also included translations of some of Apollonius's lost books on geometry known previously only from second-hand Arab and Byzantine sources. He soon became a respected establishment figure, but his relationship with Flamsteed never improved. By now Newton was also at loggerheads with the Astronomer Royal over the tardiness of his submission of observations made at Greenwich. Flamsteed blamed Halley for the breach with Newton. He wrote: 'Mr Halley has set the Master of the Mint at distance from me by false suggestions.'

The final straw came after the Royal Society appointed Halley as editor when they published Flamsteed's Greenwich star catalogue the *Historia Celeste*. This was again because Flamsteed himself had been tardy in submitting it for publication. Pigheadedly Flamsteed refused to co-operate with Halley, and as a consequence the published catalogue was full of inaccuracies. In 1713, Halley was elected one of the Secretaries of the Royal Society. Then, on 31 December 1719, Flamsteed died. Halley's name was immediately put forward 'as the fittest Person to do Honour to the Post of Astronomer Royal . . . which his Majesty was accordingly pleas'd to give him'.

Halley remained in office as Astronomer Royal until he died in 1742; he also retained his professorship at Oxford.

In later years he was involved in several disputes with Newton who, since his appointment as President of the Royal Society, often acted like a despot to his friends and enemies alike. Halley was soon in trouble with Newton for the same reasons Flamsteed had been – for holding back his observations of the Moon. Halley defended his actions vigorously on the grounds of self-interest. He was not prepared to release observations that might allow another person to anticipate his own work in trying to discover an accurate method of determining longitude at sea (using the Moon's shift across the stars) and claim the substantial prize offered by Parliament. It was over this very question of lunar observations they are reputed to have exchanged heated words a few days previous to Newton's death in 1727, and it was this incident which Thomas Hearne reported as 'a great Quarrel [which] happened between him [Newton] & Dr Halley so as they fell to bad language'. Hearne, with his usual desire to show Halley in the poorest possible light, added: 'This 'tis thought so much discomforted Sir Isaac as to hasten his end.'

Halley kept working almost to his last breath. Apart from a stroke in the latter part of 1736, which caused a slight paralysis of his right hand, he remained comparatively active even in old age.[2] After Newton's death he was promoted to the grand old man of British science. Unlike Newton, he was never knighted. Newton had earned his knighthood for his work at the Mint; to honour scientists with knighthoods in the eighteenth century for their abstruse investigations into the laws of God was almost unknown. Apart from the mild stroke, he enjoyed excellent heath, but we read that the old man 'never eat Thing but Fish, for he had no Teeth'. His end came in his eighty-sixth year on 14 June 1742, sixteen years before the comet he had predicted would return was due. Friends report that after savouring a glass of wine he expired in his chair without so much as a groan.

*   *   *

Although Halley published his *Synopsis* in 1705, comets in later years were never far from his thoughts. Other comets besides those he had seen in 1680-1 and 1682 might be brought to heel. In 1722 he was making enquiries about Michael Maestlin's observations of the bright comet of 1580 made in Bantang with which he wished to compare observations made by Tycho Brahe as the two differed. In Halley's *Tabulae Astronomicae*, published after his death in 1749, just ten years before the return of the 1682 comet (again reprinted in 1752 with an appended English translation) Halley refers back to his earlier prediction in emphatic terms: '. . . You see, therefore an agreement of all the elements in these three, which would be next to a miracle if they were three different Comets; or, if it was not the approach of the same comet towards the Sun and Earth in three different revolutions, in an ellipsis around them. Wherefore, if according to what we have already said, it should return again about the year 1758, candid posterity will not refuse to acknowledge that this was first discovered by an Englishman.'

Englishmen like Newton and Halley had cracked the secrets of cometary movement, but as the time drew nearer for the promised reappearance of the 1682 comet, its fortunes were to pass into the hands of their old rivals across the Channel – the French.

Notes

[1] In respect to Halley's political affiliations we learn from Thomas Hearne he is alleged to have told him: 'I am for the King in possession. If I am protected I am content . . .' Hearne claimed that Halley masqueraded as a Tory, but was a Whig at heart, and this has a ring of truth about it. He was certainly no revolutionary and he likely felt indifferent, if not contemptuous, about Parliamentary affairs as many free-thinking scientists do today.

[2] According to a note by Hearne, Halley was already lame in 1721 and feeling his years. He supposedly told Hearne (circa 1721) he only wished to live another seven years in order to finish a work he had begun. Whether Halley was referring to his *Astronomical Tables* or his unfinished new edition of Ptolemy's *Geography* is unknown. After completing two volumes of the latter, Halley gave up the project on hearing someone in Europe was doing the same thing. It seems Halley by this time had lost much of his former drive.

5 · A Prediction Fulfilled

HILE NEWTON'S *Principia* was hailed by most Englishmen as a masterpiece, at least on the recommendation of those who understood it, many French savants and other continentals stubbornly remained loyal to Cartesian vortices as an explanation of gravity.

Even at Cambridge, Cartesian philosophy had a toehold as part of the traditional curriculum well into the late 1690s, but it was the French Academy of Sciences which played the major role in ignoring Newton's ideas.[1] One reason was that the doctrine of vortices was designed as an escape clause from Copernicanism to satisfy orthodox Catholic prejudice. Another factor was, of course, it was the work of a Frenchman!

In France, for a time, there seems to have been a strong desire among savants to discredit Newton's theories at any cost. Not until Newton's prediction that the Earth should be sensibly flattened at its poles was verified in 1735 by two French expeditions to Lapland and Peru did consensus opinion in the French Academy swing in his favour.

By now, however, the Academy for its continued stubbornness had become the laughing-stock of Europe and the butt of British mockery. Old diehards like Bernard De Fontenelle, President of the Academy, refused to change his views no matter what colleagues like Pierre De Maupertuis, leader of the Lapland party, and one of his assistants, Alexis Claude Clairaut, told him to the contrary. However, Fontenelle proved to be the last voice in a lost cause when in 1752, in his ninety-fifth year, he published his final treatise on Cartesian vortices. Fate decreed it was to be Clairaut, with the help of two others, who would return honour to France in 1758, a year after De Fontenelle died . . .

*   *   *

It is ironic that while Newton had provided the new celestial mechanics, he had, unwittingly, handicapped his own countrymen for generations afterwards with his version of the differential calculus. Compared with the notation invented by Gottfried Leibniz, Newton's was much inferior. Newton and Halley were probably the only men able to use Newtonian notation with any facility. Succeeding Englishmen, as partizan and stubborn as their colleagues across the Channel, were no match for the continental mathematicians using Leibniz's method.

Although enlightened French mathematicians eventually adopted Newtonian mechanics, they had the good sense to discard Newtonian notation, finding it clumsy and inappropriate. As a result Newtonian mechanics was only properly developed by French mathematicians such as Clairaut, Leonhard Euler, Joseph Louis Lagrange and Pierre Simon De Laplace. The misplaced devotion to Newton's notation by Englishmen was to retard the progress of science and mathematics in England for the next century.

As 1758 approached and the comet's predicted rendezvous with the Sun, there were some still sceptical of Halley's bold claim. Others had predicted returns of comets since. Not to be outdone by an Englishman, Jacques Bernoulli, a member of the famous family of mathematicians and scientists, had announced the return of the comet 1680-1 for precisely 17 May 1719 and stated it would appear in the constellation of Libra. When no bright comet was confirmed, there were mutterings that mathematicians were no better than astrologers.

As the eighteenth century progressed, a band of French savants became convinced that *Principia* was the work of a unique genius and that Halley, as the disciple of Newton, was also a genius in his own right. Except for stubborn, old Academicians such as De Fontenelle, opinion had now swung against Cartesianism. If Halley's prediction came true, it was recognized this would be the final proof required to hammer the last nail in the coffin of the theory of vortices.

Prior to 1758, Clairaut in particular had been thinking out methods to refine Halley's calculations so as to fix more exactly the time of the comet's reappearance. A brilliant mathematician from youth, Clairaut had been admitted to the French Academy of Sciences when just eighteen years old. In 1743 he had earned himself a formidable reputation for his mathematical study on the figure of the Earth. The prize he now sought was a thorough understanding of the motion of the comet the Englishman had predicted would return.

Because he was pressed for time, Clairaut enlisted the help of the astronomer Joseph De Lalande. He too had risen brilliantly and at the time in question held the appointment of Royal Astronomer to the French court. A second helper enlisted was Madame Lepaute, born Nicole-Reine Étable de la Brière.

Madame Lepaute was the wife of a highly skilled clockmaker. As a girl she had been raised within the shadow of the Luxembourg Palace in sight of the observatory. Even at an early age she was renowned for her intelligence and wit. An anecdote from her childhood recounts that one day when a vain sister remarked to her: 'I am the fairest in the family,' Nicole is said to have countered quickly: 'Maybe so, but I am the cleverest!'

Madame Lapaute became known to Lalande when her husband made a remarkable clock with only a single wheel. As the representative of the Academy of Sciences, Lalande went to visit him and inspect the unique mechanism.

Lalande was so struck by the intelligence of the clockmaker's wife and her abilities with figures that when Clairaut revealed his plans to investigate the orbit of the expected comet and enlisted his aid, he in turn immediately enlisted the help of Madame Lepaute. So great was the undertaking they embarked upon that Lalande later revealed it was doubtful he and Clairaut would ever have finished 'had it not been for Nicole'.

The task before them was formidable. Halley had roughly estimated that the time of the comet arriving at its perihelion next time round would be at least one year longer than the interval between the two preceding returns. The new trio now strived for more exactness.

According to Lalande, they toiled incessantly, excepting meal-times, day and night, week after week, month after month. Unlike Halley, who had only approximated the influence of Jupiter, they calculated the perturbing effects of Saturn as well. It was necessary to compute the distance of the comet from both disturbing planets, not only from 1682 but also for the previous revolution – a period totalling more than 150 years. While this part was itself a laborious undertaking, it did not compare with the work of computing the disturbing force of each planet for the same period. Their task was handicapped by their ignorance of two yet undiscovered planets, Uranus and Neptune. Afterwards Lalande wrote that he found the strain of work intolerable and it permanently undermined his health.

Even before Clairaut announced their findings, the astronomers of France were busy with their telescopes. Voltaire tells us that during 1758, observers did not go to bed for fear of missing the comet. English mathematics and astronomy were in the doldrums. If there were to be honour, it would be all French.

On both sides of the Channel there were scoffers. In 1758, in London, the *Gentleman's Magazine* published verses expressing disbelief about Halley's prediction. In France, the critics through 1758 kept asking where the elusive comet was hiding, and Clairaut was driven to comment: 'The comet which has been expected for more than a year has become the subject of a curiosity much more lively than that which the public usually bestows upon questions of astronomy. True lovers of science desire its return because it would afford striking confirmation of a system in favour of which nearly all phenomena furnish conclusive evidence. Those on the contrary, who would like to see its philosophers embarrassed and at fault, hope it will not return, and that the discoveries of Newton and his partisans may prove to be on a level with the hypotheses which are the result of imagination. Several people of this class are already triumphing, and consider the delay of a year, which is due entirely to announcements destitute of all foundations, sufficient reasons for condemning the Newtonians . . . Therefore, I have undertaken to show that this delay predicted by Halley, far from invalidating the system of universal gravitation, is a necessary consequence arising from it; that it will continue yet longer and I endeavour to assign its limit.'

In November 1758 the trio's work was complete. By the 14th the findings were in the hands of the French Academy. In spite of the monumental calculations, the exact time of the comet's reappearance was still necessarily uncertain. The known periods were quite unequal: from 1531 to 1607 the interval was 27,811 days; from 1607 to 1682 it was 27,325 days, which gives a difference of 459 days between perihelion passages round the Sun. During the calculations the question to be answered was: would the new period be shorter or longer – or would it be the old value?

The concrete results of the trio's work was a prediction that the perihelion passage would be delayed for 618 days, and the actual year would be 1759. Saturn would delay the comet for 100 days and Jupiter 518 days, bringing the perihelion passage approximately to the middle of the month of April 1759. Clairaut added that probably due to terms omitted (Uranus and Neptune not discovered until 1781 and 1846 respectively) and possibly errors in calculation, there might still be a difference of one month either side of the predicted date.

An eagle-eyed French astronomer who had not gone to bed during 1758 for fear of missing the comet was Charles Messier, a civil servant employed at the Marine Observatory in Paris. Unfortunately his hopes of seeing the comet first were dashed when the returning wanderer was spotted by an obscure amateur astronomer living at Prohlis, near Dresden. This man was a farmer called George Palitzsch who saw it on the evening of Christmas Day 1758 through a telescope of just over 2 metres focal length.

Little is known about this Saxon amateur astronomer, except he was a dedicated student of the subject and possessed a very keen eyesight. So acute was his vision he was able to see with the naked eye all four of Jupiter's brightest moons. During the nineteenth century a splendid water-colour of the rosy-cheeked Farmer Palitzsch used to hang in pride of place on the walls of an observatory in Prague, but unfortunately this now seems to have disappeared[2].

After Palitzsch the next to see it was a Dr Hoffman on 28 December; then another observer in Leipzig found it on 18 January 1759. Messier's own search for the elusive object was hampered by cloud, and he did not see it until 21 January, after that he followed it for several nights. It was consequent to Messier's own discovery that a remarkable thing happened. The Observatory Director, J.N. Delisle, to whom Messier was assistant, refused to allow him to disclose his own discovery to other French savants. As a result, since communication about the other discoveries was delayed, Messier was the only French astronomer to follow it before it disappeared into the Sun's rays on its way to perihelion on 13 March 1759.

By the end of February the comet was already too close to the Sun to be visible. It was not until the last week in March it reappeared.

On its reappearance it was first seen in the southern hemisphere on 26 March by La Nux on the Isle of Bourbon (Réunion) and in Europe by Messier on the 31st. At this time it was only visible in morning twilight when it hung very low near the horizon shining like a very bright star with a tail extending over 25° in length.

Now Delisle decided to withdraw his interdict, and a formal

announcement about the reappearance of the comet was made on 1 April 1759. Delisle's censorship of his assistant's earlier observations was remarkable. We know nothing of his motivations. When Messier's earlier sightings were published, some members of the French Academy treated them as forgeries. In the end Messier's name was cleared, but the episode was never forgotten, and it followed Delisle to the end of his life.

Clairaut revised his calculations and reduced the error of prediction to nineteen days. Later the astronomer Laplace showed that had Clairaut known the true value for the mass of Saturn, the error could have been reduced to thirteen days – this without taking account of other, yet unknown, factors.

During April 1759 the comet became widely visible and was seen throughout Europe, but towards the end of the month it was difficult to follow because of its low position. It was best seen by La Nux on the Isle of Bourbon and by the Jesuit astronomer Father Coeurdoux at Pondicherry in India.

On 5 May its tail stretched to over 47° and it was very conspicuous. It was last seen by Messier on 3 June when it was still plainly visible to the naked eye, but northern observers were hampered by poor visibility. The last view of it is attributed to Chevalier, observing from Lisbon on 22 June as the comet now began retreating to the outer realms of the solar system.

The perihelion of the comet had taken place just thirty-two days before the time calculated by Clairaut and his two helpers. Their work had vindicated Newton's *Principia* and Halley's method in predicting the return of the comet. Cartesianism was dead and buried. Clairaut and his helpers had demonstrated that over an interval of 150 years of orbital motion, man could predict to within thirty-two days the position of a wandering body only visible for a short interval as it rendezvoused with the Sun.

As Lalande himself wrote when he enthused over the triumph: 'This universe beholds this year the most satisfactory phenomenon ever presented to us by astronomy; an event which, unique until this day, changes our doubts to certainty and our hypotheses to demonstration . . . M. Clairaut asked one month's grace for the theory; the month's grace was just sufficient, and the comet has appeared after a period of 586 days longer than the previous time of revolution, and thirty-two days before the time fixed; but what are thirty-two days to an interval of more than 150 years, during only one two-hundredth part of which observations were made, the comet being out of sight all the rest of the time? What are thirty days for all the other attractions of the solar system which have not been included; for all the comets, the situation and masses of which are unknown to us; for the resistance of the ethereal medium, which we are unable even to estimate, and for those quantities which of necessity have been neglected in the approximations of the calculation? . . . A difference of 586 days between the revolutions of the same comet, a difference produced by the disturbing action of Jupiter and Saturn, affords a more striking demonstration of the great principle of attractions than we could have dared to hope for, and places this law amongst the number of the fundamental truths of physics, the reality of which is no more possible to doubt than the existence of the bodies which produce it.'

Lalande also took opportunity of expressing gratitude to Mme Lepaute, for without her, he admitted, 'the work was of such drudgery to be almost impossible'. Clairaut comes off in poorer light. Although in private he was very grateful for her help – remarking 'her enthusiasm was boundless' and referred to her as 'la savante calculatric' ('the learned computer') – he suppressed a public tribute to her in his book on Halley's comet (*Théorie des Comètes*, 1760). This was to please, so the story goes, a woman who was jealous of the superior ability of Nicole Lepaute; or, as Lalande puts it 'a woman who was full of pretensions to knowledge without any sort of foundation'.

Lalande tells us that this other woman 'succeeded in bringing about injustice' through 'a wise but weak scholar of whom she had made a conquest'. As a postscript Lalande concludes: 'There are so few of these superior women that others have been quite successful in hiding what these unusual women know.'

Lalande, however, made sure Nicole Lepaute earned her due. When he was placed in charge of the French almanac (the *Connaissance des Temps*), she became one of his chief assistants.[3]

Messier, disappointed at not being the first to rediscover Halley's comet and thus bring double honour to France, reaped his share of rewards in the years following. He became besotted by comets to the point of monomania and made them his life's work. When Delisle retired as director of the observatory in 1761, Messier was promoted to take his place. He was a man with no inclination for mathematics or for theory – for him astronomy was the joy of observing under the canopy of stars. His first comet discovery came on the morning of 26 January 1760; and through the years he went on to make seventeen more discoveries, some of which were also found independently by his rivals. The French became the great comet hunters of the age, and their keen rivalry a legend. So successful was Messier he earned the nickname 'the Ferret'. Another title given him, according to Delambre, was 'bird-nester' of comets, who quoted the words used by Louis XV in a eulogy on Messier in 1818. Perhaps the best-known anecdote concerning his dedication to comets records that after he had found his twelfth comet and was searching for his thirteenth, his wife fell ill and died. During the last few days of her life, while Messier was busy taking care of her and he was unable to observe, his rival Montaigne of Limoges discovered a comet. After the funeral, when a friend offered condolences about his bereavement, Messier was overheard to remark: 'Alas, Montaigne has robbed me of my thirteenth comet!' Then, realizing what answer was really expected, he quickly added: 'Ah! Poor woman.' A postscript to the anecdote tells us that his wife was soon forgotten, but his grieving for the lost comet continued to cause anguish and suffering.

Notes

[1] It often comes as a surprise to students of the history of science to discover that six years after the publication of *Principia*, in 1687, Cartesian philosophy was still in vogue and being taught in Cambridge. This we have on the authority of Whiston who took over Newton's Lucasian Chair in Mathematics in 1703. Whiston relates that circa 1693 'We at *Cambridge*, poor Wretches, were ignominiously studying the fictitious Hypotheses of the Cartesian, which Sir *Isaac Newton* had also himself done formerly, as I have heard him say'.

Earlier in the same passage Whiston tells us: 'After I had taken Holy Orders [1693], I returned to the College, and went on with my Studies there particularly Mathematics, and Cartesian Philosophy; which was alone in Vogue with us at that Time. But it was not long before I, with immense Pains, but no Assistance, set myself with the utmost Zeal to the Study of Sir *Isaac Newton's* wonderful Discoveries in his *Philosophiae Naturalis Principia Mathematica*, one or two of which Lectures I had heard him read in the publick schools, though I understood them not at all at this Time . . .'

Whiston, as we know, was not alone as a Cambridge scholar in not understanding Newton. In addition to this, Newton was out of sympathy with the general trend of thought in Cambridge where few properly understood him or his ideas. This was a factor in persuading Newton to leave his academic seclusion for the crowded life and the fleshpots of the metropolis and take up an appointment as Warden of the Mint in 1696.

[2] Johann 'George' Palitzsch (1723-1788) is sometimes portrayed as an ignorant rustic with little learning, but the opposite is the case. He was a gentleman by birth and had many diverse scientific interests, including an expertise in botany and lightning conductors. His library is said to have consisted of 3,500 volumes. While the Seven Years War raged all round Dresden, he buried his telescopes for safe keeping and only disintered his 'seven-foot' instrument in order to search for Halley's comet. After he rediscovered the comet in 1758, he became a celebrated figure and corresponded with the leading societies in Europe and individually with many astronomers, including William Herschel. He is remembered today by a monument in Prohlis.

[3] Lalande and Mme Lepaute subsequently worked together for many years. We can suspect that the astronomer was smitten and a little in love with his bright assistant, nine years older than himself. He tells us: 'although she was not pretty Mme Lepaute had a good share of the qualities of her sex – an elegant figure, a pretty little foot, and such a beautiful hand that M Voirot, painter to the King, after finishing her portrait asked permission to copy the hand in order to have a model of the loveliest kind to use for other paintings.' The picture took pride of place in Lalande's study, with the added compliment by him that it was hung beside a very rare portrait of Copernicus.

It is doubtful if Mme Lepaute was ever Lalande's mistress, for he hints she was devoted to her husband who 'had regard for her that was mingled with awe'.

Reading between the lines, Lalande tells us he was also a little envious of the clockmaker husband who had such a paragon of a wife – whose 'good taste and elegance characterized everything about her without detracting from her studies', and whose household account books 'were a model of perfection and stood with her astronomical tables'. While their intimacy stopped short of their being lovers, there was, however, a strong cameraderie between them, for he reveals: 'she drew me away from dangerous alliances; she brought me into a circle of pleasant, well-educated people; she suffered my faults and helped me overcome them. The times I spent with her and her family are those I like best to recall, and this memory spreads a gentleness over the last years of my life as her friendship gave charm to my youth.'

When the clockmaker became crippled, Nicole Lepaute devoted the last seven years of her life to his care, sacrificing all her academic work. It must have been a sad blow when Lalande heard she had caught typhoid. She died on 6 December 1788, predeceasing her husband by a few months.

6 · The Return of 1835-6

AS MAY BE EXPECTED, the triumphant return of Halley's comet in 1758-9 stimulated a great interest in comets generally. Halley's prediction, based on mathematics rather than astrology, had been fulfilled; Newton's methods had been improved upon by Clairaut with the help of other savants. Halley's comet could now be put aside, for those who had observed it this time round would be dead when it returned in 1835. It was time to concentrate on bringing other comets into line to show that Halley's wasn't an exception to the rule of comets.

The first task was to identify other comets of short period. Halley himself had nicknamed the 1682 comet 'the Mercury among comets' in an allusion to the swiftness of the innermost planet on its journey round the Sun. Compared with the 1680-1 comet, to which he had assigned a period of 575 years – inferring this was the same comet seen before in 1106, 531 and 43 BC – Halley's comet was one of relatively short period. But were there comets with even shorter periods so astronomers would not have to wait interminably to see them again in order to check out their theory of periodicity? While the orbits of other comets were calculated, and some early returns predicted, it was several decades later before a sure answer was forthcoming.

Meanwhile the task of collecting information and cataloguing past comet apparitions, as Halley had done, continued. Foremost among the scholars devoted to this study was the French astronomer Alexandre-Guy Pingré, who was born in Paris in 1711. At sixteen he entered a scholastic order; by the age of twenty-four he held a professorship in theology, but then a purge by the Jesuits deposed him. It was not until he was thirty-eight he was offered an astronomer's position. Like Halley, he made a number of scientific voyages. Later in life, again like Halley, he was able to return to his Alma Mater where he published his masterwork in two volumes in 1783-4.

Its full title is *Cométographie; ou Traité historique et théorique des Comètes* and it provides a source-book – a veritable bible – for all aspects of cometary astronomy up to his time. In spite of the two centuries since its inception, Pingré's *Cométographie* remains the best available work on the subject and is never likely to be surpassed. Without its help as a reference source we should be much less well informed about comets that appeared before the eighteenth century.

Pingré drew on all the records of those who had gone before him, including what was gleaned from China. It is the early Chinese annals – later translated more comprehensively by others after Pingré – which today provide the best comet sources before European Medieval times.

*   *   *

In the second half of the eighteenth century the search for new comets of short period continued. With few exceptions most of the new comets were generally dim objects seen at the very limit of naked-eye visibility or only to be identified through telescopes. One exception to the run of undistinguished comets was that seen in 1769, discovered telescopically by Messier on 8 August. When first sighted it was just at the limit of naked-eye visibility, but by 28 August it had become a brilliant object with a tail extending to 48°. On 10 September, La Nux, on the Isle of Bourbon, traced out its tail to a length of 90° to 98° and remarked it was an extremely bright object. In later years Messier was to remember this particular comet discovery of his with a special reverence for his hero – Napoleon.

With the application of telescopic power and a growing band of diligent searchers, discoveries increased in numbers over those of previous centuries. Between 1601 and 1700, thirty-five comets had been seen, between 1701 and 1800, the number more than doubled to seventy-three, and most of these fell to comet hunters in the second half of the century. From 1801 to 1900, the number of comets leapt to 335 . . .

*   *   *

By the second half of the eighteenth century comets had been recognized for many years as significant cosmic bodies. How significant in terms of mass and size no one yet knew. It was generally agreed, however, the Earth's collision with a comet might have dire consequences. Much of this thinking referred back to 1696 when William Whiston had published a book entitled *A New Theory of the Earth*. Whiston had in fact borrowed heavily on Halley's earlier ideas and in his book elaborated on the theme that all past geological upheavals recorded in the scriptures were the results of the Earth's encounter with a comet. The comet in question was none other than that of 1680-1 to which Halley had assigned a period of 575 years.

Halley claimed that the 1680-1 comet was likely the same as the one seen in 1106, 531 and 43 BC after the death of Caesar. Whiston, however, extended its alleged apparitions back to 2344 BC and 2919 BC. The two later dates were significant as they had been fixed by Church chronologists as choice dates for the Mosaic deluge.

Once Whiston had embarked on his historical-pseudo-scientific romance, his imagination knew no bounds. Even the Earth itself was identified as an ancient comet, but the nub of his theory was that the 1680-1 comet was dispatched by God at a previous apparition 'to inflict an awful punishment on man for his sins'. The result was that, at God's command, the tail of this 'prodigious' comet wrapped itself round the Earth and caused the oceans to sweep away and drown the planet's guilty inhabitants 'in a glorious religious purge'.

For a time Whiston's book was given a scientific accolade. In public fame it temporarily eclipsed Newton's *Principia*. It was quoted in the style of exaggerated puffs common at that time as 'the noblest production of genius and science that had ever been given the world'. The book created a furore, even in France. Following this, others subsequently jumped on the bandwagon about comets not only as portents of disaster but as actual physical causes for them. The catastrophe idea fostered by Whiston was still firmly engrained in the public's mind when in 1773 a rumour swept Paris and then all of France that a comet was about to strike the Earth. Had not the famous Academician Lalande just announced this!

When Lalande, now at the peak of his fame, was told of what had happened, he was astonished. What had started as an innocent announcement by him that he was to present a paper before the Academy on 21 April entitled 'Reflections on the approach of a comet to the Earth' had clearly been misunderstood. Now the public and the media were convinced that a new comet was shortly to cut across the Earth's track and collide with it. Indeed the firm dates fixed for the end of the world was 20 or 21 May.

Ironically, he had not even read the paper at the Academy's meeting on 21 April for lack of time. So great was the panic he decided he must publish a disclaimer, choosing to publish it in the *Gazette de France*.

Unfortunately, Lalande's disclaimer was not emphatic enough. It did not immediately allay fears; if anything, it confirmed to the public there was an official cover-up and the distinguished astronomer only wished to disguise the terrible truth. Lalande consequently came in for much abuse.

Lalande's paper was published in the *Comptes rendus* later in 1773. Its content, exaggerated by rumour and sufficient to spark off the earlier panic, was innocuous enough, for it principally consisted of a table of figures setting out the distances of the nodes of sixty-one comets from the Earth's orbit.

In his disclaimer to the press, Lalande made reference to a comet 'due in 18 years'. This was another of Halley's predictions about comets seen in 1532 and in 1661. According to Halley's reckoning these two comets were the same and it would return about 1788. After his success with predicting the return of the 1682 comet, astronomers were now optimistic about the verification of the periodicity of this second comet. The English astronomer Nevil Maskelyne, appointed fourth Astronomer Royal in 1765, wrote a paper in *Philosophical Transactions* for 1786 to aid its rediscovery. When the British established the new colony at Botany Bay in Eastern Australia, an officer was seconded to the expedition to make a search for it. It was not seen in the Antipodes or in Europe, and later the French Academy offered a prize to anyone who would investigate its motion. For a time the challenge was not taken up, but then P.F.A. Méchain, arch-rival to Messier as a comet hunter, undertook the calculation. The result was that the identity of the two comets of 1532 and 1661 was found not probable.

The Lalande episode was by no means an isolated case of a public comet panic. Later there were several echoes of 1773. In 1816, again in France, rumours were rife about another approaching comet, and the end of the world was fixed as 18 July. It provided the blasé with an opportunity to jest at the expense of Lalande, who had now been dead for nine years.

Three years before the scheduled reappearance of Halley's comet, another returning comet was calculated to cross the Earth's orbit, and the day of doom was fixed as 29 October 1832. In attempts to defuse the alarm raised by the rumours, F.J.D. Arago, recalling 1773 and 1816, drew up a notice to act as a disclaimer.

On this occasion Arago informed the French public that the odds for such an encounter was 281 million to one. Less reassuring news, however, was Arago's opinion that if the Earth were struck by the nucleus of a comet, it would annihilate the entire human race . . . In the light of twentieth-century knowledge we could say Arago's prediction was unduly pessimistic. In the ancient past, the Earth was most certainly struck by comets many times over; in recent times, at least once.[1]

*   *   *

The search for new comets in hope of finding one of shorter period than Halley's continued, and the French at one time held almost a monopoly in this field. Then the path of a comet discovered by Messier in 1770 was studied by Lexell in St Petersburg. He finally succeeded in calculating an orbit for it and realized it revolved in an ellipse round the Sun in a period of just over 5½ years. Unfortunately, by the time the tedious calculations were complete, the orbit of the comet had carried it close to Jupiter whose

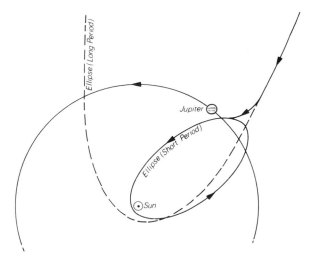

Fig. 8 Jupiter plays a significant role in capturing comets. Comets with orbits of long and indeterminate periods may be transformed into comets of shorter periods.

97

attracting bulk had the effect of switching it into a new path, from where it was no longer visible from the Earth at the time of its perihelion approach[2].

Some years later another new comet came under suspicion as a possible short-period candidate for study. This was a comet discovered in 1818 by the Frenchman Jean Louis Pons, who had replaced Messier as the premier comet hunter in the world. Pons proved to be the most successful comet hunter who has ever lived, and his tally of thirty-six comets has never been approached since. Pons's new comet was studied by Johann Franz Encke, who later was to investigate the comet of 1680-1 and find that Halley's period of 575 years was in error (p. 78). If Encke's calculations for the 'new' 1818 comet were correct, here was a true Mercury among comets, for its path took it round the Sun in the very short time of 3⅓ years. He was now able to identify it from its characteristic orbital fingerprints with a comet seen earlier in 1786 by Méchain, with another in 1795 by Caroline Herschel and yet another seen in 1805 when it was discovered independently by Huth in Frankfurt-on-Oder, Bouvard in Paris and Pons himself in Marseilles. Until Encke proved this was the same comet returning time and time again, it was believed these earlier comets had separate identities.

Encke calculated the 1818 comet would be at perihelion again with the Sun on 24 May 1822, and in due course it was resighted almost exactly in the place predicted[3].

This recovery of Pons's comet was now recognized as the second great milestone in the history of cometary astronomy. Another comet besides Halley's had been successfully predicted and then observed almost exactly where it should be. What was even more interesting, it proved there were comets in the solar system with short periods comparable with those of the inner planets. For his outstanding work Encke was awarded the Gold Medal of the Royal Astronomical Society in 1824, and the comet thereafter became known as Encke's comet. However, history relates that Encke himself always more modestly referred to it as 'the Comet of Pons'. In comet catalogues today it is designated P/Encke; the P prefix denotes it is periodical and a comet whose orbit is known with certainty.

Since Encke's time the comet has been observed at every apparition except one during its short 3⅓ year journey round the Sun. It was only missed at its apparition of 1944 during World War II when it was again unfavourably placed for observation in the northern hemisphere.

The recognition of this new periodic comet was to raise some interesting speculations about comets in general during the following years. Encke kept up his studies of it because some aspects of its behaviour still puzzled him. The period of its revolution round the Sun seemed to be getting shorter, not by much but by an amount still just detectable by his computing methods. In 1838 he announced the results of his findings. After taking into account every conceivable planetary perturbation, the comet had returned to its last three rendezvous with the Sun 2 ½ hours too early. After Encke's death in 1865, the comet was investigated by Von Asten at the Pulkova Observatory. He noted that on its return in 1868 its change of acceleration suddenly decreased by half. Then in 1871 any acceleration had vanished.

Later on other comets were found to have similar characteristics, but since Encke's comet comes round more frequently than any other, this example has been studied more intently. During Encke's day it was suggested a resisting medium in space was responsible for the comet's behaviour, but nowadays this idea finds little favour.[4] Acceleration characteristics have been rigorously investigated in other comets as these small but mysterious non-gravitational forces at work provide orbit computers with considerable difficulties when trying to calculate exact periods. One of the best-known examples of erratic behaviour is with Halley's comet itself . . .

*   *   *

Apart from the numerous fainter comets discovered between 1758 and 1835, a few, like Messier's comet in 1769, were as brilliant as Halley's – some much more so. The comet which appeared at the end of March 1811 proved to be one of the brightest ever seen. It developed a tail 70° in length and is said to have inspired terror in the Russian peasantry about their fate at the hands of Napoleon. In 1808, Messier had published a book entitled *La grande Comète qui apparut à la naissance de Napoléon le Grand* to uphold the idea that the bright comet he had discovered in 1769 was actually Napoleon's lucky birth comet. Now, in 1811, the Little Emperor saw the new brilliant comet as a heaven-sent, good omen for his Eastern campaign . . .

Alas for human vanity and miscalculation. While the 1811 comet apparently was of benefit in ripening the grapes for the wine harvest that year and for the prolificacy of twins, it had a souring influence on the fortunes of Napoleon; in hindsight those who recalled it in 1812 believed it had been the herald of his downfall.

*   *   *

99

As 1835 approached, it was a new opportunity to test the advances in theoretical astronomy which had occurred in the period since Halley's comet had last been seen. Although celestial mechanics had undergone many refinements after 1758, the task of predicting the exact time for the comet's next perihelion approach to the Sun was still a formidable one.

As the year drew closer, a prize worth a gold medal and 3,000 francs was offered by the Institute of France for any person who could frame up a general theory of perturbations acting on comets that could be applied to Halley's comet. For a time the challenge was not accepted, and the Institute renewed its offer several times. Computers with the necessary skill were only too aware of what dedication was required; what possible ruination of health accompanied by upsets in domestic routine such a declaration of intent would incur. The story of Clairaut, Lalande and Mme Lepaute, and their toils, had long passed into folklore.

As early as 1817 a prize was also offered by the Turin Academy for a study of the comet's perturbations since 1759. This challenge was taken up by Baron Damoiseau, and his Essay was published in 1820 in the *Memoirs of the Turin Academy*. By this time account could be taken of the effect on the comet by the massive planet Uranus which, since Clairaut's time, had been discovered by William Herschel in 1781.

The upshot was that Damoiseau fixed the comet's new perihelion passage as 20 hours Paris time 4 November 1835. Following this, another Frenchman, the Count de Pontecoulant, made an independent calculation and reached more or less the same results, except he fixed his date for perihelion at 17 hours Paris time 12 November 1835 – a little over a week later than that of his rival.

Neither Damoiseau nor Pontecoulant, however, had completed a definitive study of the comet's perturbations by all relevant planets. This more exacting and time-consuming challenge was taken up by the German astronomer Otto August Rosenberger, who earlier had served as assistant at the Königsberg Observatory under Friedrich Wilhelm Bessel – the man later to miss discovering the planet Neptune by a quirk of fate.

In undertaking his own researches, Rosenberger believed it necessary not only to account for the movements of the comet since 1759 but also to go back to study its movements from 1682 to 1758. He took into account all the perturbing effects of the massive planets Jupiter, Saturn and Uranus and also those of the inner terrestrial planets Mercury, Venus, Earth and Mars. Neither did he overlook the peculiar effects of the then supposed resisting medium which was suspected to be operating on Encke's comet. Rosenberger himself was never convinced about the reality of such a medium and therefore he decided to publish two predictions: one taking account of it and another ignoring it.

Rosenberger had the advantage over his earlier rivals of having the use of a series of previously unpublished observations made during 1759 by James Bradley, the man who had succeeded Halley as Astronomer Royal. These earlier observations passed into Bessel's possession via an astronomer called Stephen Peter Rigaud. Bessel in turn passed them on to his old protégé, Rosenberger.

Rosenberger published his results in the *Astronomische Nachrichten*, the most influential astronomical journal of the nineteenth century. With no allowance for the resisting medium, the time and date would be 0 hours Paris time on 11 November 1837; allowing for a medium the date would fall about a week earlier, at 19 hours Paris time on 3 November.

In his paper, Rosenberger detailed the effects of each individual planet on the comet: the Earth's effect was $15\frac{2}{3}$ days, Venus $5\frac{1}{3}$ days and Mercury and Mars together 1 day. Added up they equalled a total of about 22 days and would hasten the comet in its orbit by that amount.

Another German computer, Lehmann, believed there was still room for a fourth voice in the matter. Although Lehmann was not as thorough as Rosenberger, he extended his study of the orbit back to 1607. He concluded that the perihelion would take place on 26 November 1835, about two weeks later than the dates fixed by Pontecoulant's and Rosenberger's first result and three weeks later than Damoiseau's prediction and Rosenberger's second result.

The search began in 1834, at least a year before the comet's predicted perihelion. Olbers suggested there was a strong possibility of spotting it between December 1834 and April 1835 when its path lay over the constellations of Auriga and Taurus, regions of the sky very favourably placed for observers in the northern hemisphere. Waiting in the southern hemisphere, at the Cape of Good Hope, was John Herschel with his 20ft focal-length reflector – then the largest telescope in the world. This British astronomer had gone to South Africa in 1834 to extend the catalogue of objects observed by him and his father, Sir William Herschel. Because of the light-gathering power of his great telescope, many expected that in the race to spot the comet, Herschel would have a decided advantage over all others.

All the initial searches proved unfruitful. The comet continued to elude the large band of professional and amateur astronomers anxious to stamp their names on posterity as Farmer Palitzsch had done on the night of Christmas Day 1758.

One of the observatories taking part in the search was the Collegio Romano at the Vatican. It was equipped with one of the finest 15-cm telescopes in the world, and its location in the clear skies of the Mediterranean gave it an edge over its more northern rivals which had to contend with long cloud-outs sometimes lasting weeks on end. On the night of 5 August 1835 the Director of the Collegio Romano, Father Dumouchel, was putting in his stint at the telescope. After making several careful sweeps, his attention was suddenly alerted. Not far away from the position predicted by Rosenberger, near the star Zeta Tauri, was a faint, slightly misty star-like image. Applying a higher power to examine it more closely, he knew at once it must be the returning comet. It was, however, still very faint, and the position he measured for it did not please him. He saw it again on 6 August, but the first observation he wished to be used for the purpose of announcing its exact position was that of 7 August.

During the following days the presence of bright moonlight and cloudy skies prevented independent resightings of the comet elsewhere. It was not until 21 August it was picked up in another of Europe's finest telescopes at Dorpat in Russia by Friedrich Georg Wilhelm Struve, then Director of the observatory there. During the following week it was seen in turn at all the leading European observatories.

Struve's measures with the magnificent 24-cm refractor at Dorpat showed the comet only differed from Rosenberger's predicted ephemeris by 7' of arc in Right Ascension and 17' in Declination. The consequence of this difference showed that the perihelion passage would be delayed until 10.30 hours Paris time 16 November − or five days later than the date predicted by Rosenberger's estimate disallowing for a resisting medium and only four days later than the inspired, but less thoroughly researched, prediction by Pontecoulant. Afterwards it was Rosenberger who received the major accolade and he was awarded the Gold Medal of the Royal Astronomical Society in 1837.

During September 1835 the comet increased in brightness. By 23 September, Struve could just see it with the naked eye. A few days later it generally became visible without optical assistance.

As early as 24 September a rudimentary tail was noticed and during October it grew to a length of 20° to 25°, others reported it 30° long. The comet became a conspicuous object as it moved through the constellations of Ursa Major, Hercules and Ophiuchus.

In spite of his large telescope and arrays of lesser instruments, Herschel, at the Cape and out of touch with the northern hemisphere, did not spot the comet until 28 October − and then only after having been notified of it by another British astronomer, a Mr Maclear, resident at the Cape Observatory. Herschel lacked an exact ephemeris, having left England before Rosenberger's became available. However, he must have been annoyed with himself for not spotting the comet earlier, as when he did, it was already a prominent object. He later remarked: 'I am sure that I must have often swept with a night-glass over the very spot where it stood in the morning before sunrise; and never was surprise greater than mine at seeing it riding high in the sky, broadly visible to the naked eye, when pointed out to me by a note from Mr Maclear who saw it with no less amazement on the 24th.'

A few weeks later Herschel's 20-ft telescope came into its own. Using its full power, he was to make some of the best detailed examinations of a comet's head ever obtained.

Towards perihelion time the comet sank lower and lower until it disappeared below the south-west horizon. The last view of it was on 30 November. The comet remained hidden by the glare of the Sun until 31 December.

Since the 1758-9 return of Halley's comet, the number of professional and amateur astronomers had increased manyfold. So too had the power and effectiveness of telescopes. There were also many more observatories, and those like Dorpat and the Collegio Romano were equipped with instruments of exacting quality.

With the successful repeat prediction of the 1835 apparition of Halley's comet, the dynamical problems of comets appeared to be solved. All that seemed to be required was application of effort combined with the necessary mathematics and skill.

But what of the comets themselves? What were they made of? How did they differ in physical make-up from the other, apparently more solid, bodies in the solar system?

No one knew. Neither was it known for sure yet whether comets shone by their own light or whether they were only rendered visible by reflected light received from the Sun. Comets were usually observed as vague, misty objects, sometimes with a bright star-like nucleus, and it was mostly only near the Sun they began to develop their tail structures.

Before the reappearance of Halley's comet in 1835, there had been a dearth of bright comets in the years immediately preceding it. The last really bright one had appeared in 1811. Since then the puzzle about the physical nature of comets had begun to intrigue the new breed of astronomers who wished to know something beyond the dynamical qualities of bodies moving in space.

Back in 1819 the French astronomer Arago had first investigated the light of comets, using a polariscope. He chose the comet of 1819 which had suddenly appeared above the north-western horizon and was discovered independently by several people on 1 July. It was visible to the naked eye but it was nothing like as brilliant as the 1811 comet. From his observations Arago deduced that comets shone by reflected light rather than by any light intrinsic to them. His work, however, needed confirmation, and, needless to say, he was keen to apply his instrument to Halley's comet as soon as it became bright enough.

It was on 23 October 1835 he first turned his apparatus on the returned comet. The earlier results were confirmed: 'The light of the comet,' he wrote, 'is not composed of rays having properties of direct [intrinsic] light; it is reflected or polarised; that is to say definitely it is light that has proceeded [been reflected] from the Sun.'

Now at least one of the mysteries about comets seemed solved; comets were definitely akin to the planetary bodies in the solar system in that like the planets they shone by reflected light. However, it was not as simple as Arago and his contemporaries imagined. Several generations later, when the spectroscope was applied to comets, this straightforward picture was to become complicated.

Other mysteries about the physical nature of comets were the envelopes of nebulous matter often seen radiating from the regions of the coma and nucleus. Sometimes rays emerging from the leading side of the comet seemed to have been forced backwards by the action of the Sun. Drawings of very bright comets made in the past had occasionally shown this, particularly some by Hevelius, but later observers believed them to be exaggerated features or downright distortions of truth. Earlier observers had also reported that bright undulations or coruscations were often seen to pass down along the tails of comets. Now there was hope that Halley's comet would shed information on the reality of these features.

After Herschel finally picked up the comet in October 1835, he observed it assiduously on every possible occasion through his 20-ft telescope. He described his astonishment at the changes that took place in the comet from hour to hour and from night to night. Jets, or hoods, of luminous material were ejected from the nuclear region, and its appearance was in a state of flux. On 28 October he described the comet: 'Within the well-defined head and somewhat eccentrically placed was seen a vividly luminous nucleus, or rather an object which I know no better way to describe than by calling it a miniature comet having a nucleus, head and a tail of its own perfectly distinct and considerably exceeding in intensity the nebular disc or envelope.'

Herschel's observations were to confirm the very tenuous nature of cometary heads when he noted that a very faint star, over which the comet's head was passing, remained quite undiminished in brightness even though it was within 40″ of the nucleus.

Earlier, during the first week in October, Struve was observing the central regions of the head with his fine Fraunhofer refractor. He noted the nucleus appeared like a fan-shaped flame emanating from a bright point; then it took the form of an oblong red-hot coal. By 13 October, he reported the centre of the comet looked like 'a stream of fire issuing from a cannon's mouth after discharge when the sparks are driven backwards as by a violent wind'. At times he believed the flame to be in motion 'similar to the flickering of the Aurora Borealis'. Then a second small flame, or jet, was seen. By 5 November the comet's head was shaped like a 'powder horn' and arched in a remarkable way.

One of the father-figures of British observational astronomy, Admiral William Henry Smyth, then Captain, saw and drew much the same thing. On 10 October, he had noted: 'The comet in this evening's examination presented an extraordinary phenomenon. The brush, fan, or gleam of light was clearly perceptible issuing from the nucleus . . . On viewing this appearance, it was impossible not to recall the strange drawing of the 'luminous sector' which is given by Hevelius in his *Annus Climactericus* as the representation of Halley's comet in 1682 and which has been considered a distortion.'

Other observers were also describing the remarkable activity in the head, and it was widely noted that the comet alternatively lost and regained a tail. The head of the comet would contract so it almost resembled a star, then, a few nights later, it would be swelled out into a milky-white nebulous globe which over the following nights would gradually dissolve again and finally vanish.

Bessel, observing from Königsberg, made a famous series of drawings illustrating the changes from night to night. He was also beginning to suspect that 'the emission of the tail' was due to 'a purely electrical phenomenon' operative between the Sun and the head of the comet. He was on the right track, but his idea was not to be confirmed for more than a century until the solar wind was discovered during the 1950s.

When the comet reappeared in January 1836, after its close approach to the Sun, it was still a noteworthy sight, It now passed into the far southern skies and began to fade as it retreated from the Sun. It was still visible to the naked eye in mid-February. The last view of it was by John Herschel in May 1836. It was now low in the sky and an object about magnitude 9 or 10. The big telescope could not be depressed low enough to follow it so it was watched through an auxiliary refracting telescope of 10-cm aperture.

It is of interest that this same small telescope, through which the last view of the comet was glimpsed in 1836, was many years later attached to another telescope at Helwan in Egypt to act as a finder; and it was the Helwan telescope that first photographed the comet unknowingly when it reappeared in 1909 . . .

Notes

[1] The Tunguska 'meteorite' event which occurred in Siberia on 30 June 1908 was probably the result of the Earth encountering a small comet or remnant of a comet that had approached from the direction of the Sun and therefore was unseen before impact. While a truly definitive account of this unusual event – based on firm evidence rather than speculation – still remains to be written, enigmatic clues point towards a cometary origin rather than any other.

At the present time it is scientifically fashionable to cite many past Earth catastrophes as being due to impacts by comets in the tradition of Halley and Whiston. The demise of the dinosaurs and other difficult-to-explain biological extinctions occurring in the geological record have also been attributed to impacts by comets, giant meteorites or asteroids. While these theories are plausible and interesting, they are nevertheless based on the slenderest evidence and/or colourful speculation. For the most part these ideas are formulated by people who favour 'catastrophe theory ' in relation to changing events in the Earth's past rather than by the gradualists who still advocate the doctrine of uniformitarianism first fostered by the eighteenth-century geologist James Hutton. The general reader, as well as the working scientist, needs to be ever mindful of Finagle's mischievous, but wholly apposite, Laws of Science: Science is truth: don't be misled by facts/No matter what result is anticipated, there is always someone willing to fake it/No matter what the result, there is always someone eager to misinterpret it/No matter what occurs, there is always someone who believes it happened according to his pet theory.

[2] On 1 July 1770, Lexell's comet approached the Earth within 1,200,000 km – the closest approach made by any *known* comet. It appeared to observers over $2\frac{1}{2}°$ in diameter – or five times the apparent diameter of the full Moon.

3 Because the comet at this apparition would be invisible to observers in the north, it was necessary to look for it in the southern hemisphere. At this time the only observatory in regular use in the southern hemisphere was at Parramatta in New South Wales. It belonged to the Governor, Sir Thomas Brisbane, who was often accused by his political opponents of too much concern for astronomy to the detriment of his political duties. On Sir Thomas's staff at this time was the astronomer George Rumker who was very interested in comets. In due course, armed with Encke's ephemeris, Rumker began his search and shortly after found it on 2 June 1822 in the position predicted.

4 The erratic behaviour of Encke's comet has been subject to many researches. Since, as far as is known, it is the comet with the shortest period, it might be expected to wear out more quickly owing to the frequency with which it is subject to the erosive bombardment by the solar wind at close quarters. The comet is subject to marked variations in brightness between apparitions and before and after perihelion. However, judging by its present behaviour it shows little evidence that it will wear out over the next century as some previously suggested it might do. When at some unknown earlier period it was captured from a long-period orbit into its smaller present-day ($3\frac{1}{3}$-year) orbit (via the method illustrated in Fig. 8) it was probably a much larger comet than it is today. Since its capture, it must have suffered several major disruptions. Part of the debris is seen annually in the display of the Beta Taurid meteors occurring about 30 June each year. It has been suggested that one of the more sizeable chunks which broke off the comet, and then later encountered the Earth, was the mysterious object that caused the famous Tunguska event in 1908 *(see note above)*. Another interesting suggestion links Encke's comet with the asteroid 2212 Hephaistos as both objects have very similar orbits.

7 · From Halley to Hastings

FTER HALLEY had identified the comet of 1682 as the reappearance of one seen earlier in 1607 and 1531, others made attempts to extend his work even further back. Halley himself had tentatively identified the year 1456 as another likely possibility, but he was not sure. The comets of 1531, 1607 and 1682 had given him intervals of 76 and 75 years. On this evidence alone a great comet should have appeared about the year 1456, and it just so happened that one was seen at the time the Turks were threatening to overrun Europe.

Had Halley had access to the observations of Paolo Toscanelli, the Florentine cosmographer, he would certainly have used them to include the apparition of 1456 in his schema to extend observations back in time. Toscanelli was the only European to make useful observations of the comet at this apparition when he recorded its path among the stars and described it as follows: 'Its head was round and as large as the eye of an ox, and from it issued a tail fan-shaped like that of a peacock. Its tail was prodigious, for it trailed through a third of the firmament.'

Toscanelli's observations were not positional observations in the modern sense but a plotted diagram of the comet's path in respect to neighbouring stars. Unfortunately this diagram remained unknown until Giovanni Celoria discovered it in the nineteenth century and was able to deduce from it an orbit for *a* comet. Celoria was unaware this might be

Halley's comet, but Schulhof noticed it bore a very strong resemblance to the orbital elements and a sure identity was soon firmly established.

Even with his study of the 1607 apparition seen by Kepler in Prague, Halley's observational sources were limited. Indeed, it is ironic that Halley was acquainted with observations made in distant Prague but quite unaware of those made by an Englishman a short carriage-ride from the City of London. This English observer was Thomas Harriot who first saw the comet from Sion House near Isleworth, on the western outskirts of London, on 21 September 1607 when he measured its position with a cross-staff, giving the off-set distance of the comet's nucleus from various stars. He followed the comet from night to night, and his last observation is dated 13 October when the tail he describes was 'obscurissima'.

Halley was also unaware of the observations made by Harriot's friend and correspondent Sir William Lower in the West Country. Lower sent an account of them in a letter dated 30 September addressed 'to his especiall good friend Mr. Thomas Harriotte alt Sion neere London'.

Lower tells he first saw the comet at 'Illford combe' (the old name for Ilfracombe). However, in a later passage in the letter it implies he had embarked on a ship bound for Wales when at about midnight he saw the comet. Later he observed it again at a place called Traventi, where he had an estate through marriage. Lower also used a surveyor's cross-staff of the type then in vogue for measuring land. From 22 September to 6 October he observed the comet on every occasion excepting four nights when the sky was cloudy and one night when he confesses charmingly he 'was a gossipinge'.

Harriot's and Lower's observations remained unknown until they fell into the hands of Baron von Zach, one of the most influential writers on astronomy round about the turn of the nineteenth century. The story goes that the Baron visited England in 1784 on a tour, and because the person concerned knew of his profound interests in historical papers, he gave him a bundle of forgotten manuscripts belonging to Thomas Harriot, a celebrated seventeenth century mathematician, who had remained very obscure. The Baron realized that in his grasp was a prize indeed. These were priceless documents which shed further light on the life and works of two totally forgotten English worthies – Harriot and Lower.

Unfortunately the Baron's English was poor and subsequently he made some wrong assumptions about authorship. He attributed a letter actually written by Sir William Lower to Harriot as coming from Henry Percy, Earl of Northumberland (patron of Harriot) during the time he was held a state prisoner in The Tower of London in 1610.

In due course the 'deciphered' manuscripts were published by the Baron in the *Berliner Astronomisches Jahrbuch* for 1788 and later papers in the *Monatliche Correspondenz*. Fortunately the errors were spotted by Rigaud, who gave a corrected version of them in the Appendix to his now classic *Miscellaneous Works and Correspondence of the Rev James Bradley* published in 1832.

Halley's sources for the 1531 apparition were those of Peter Apian (Petrus Apianus) of Ingolstadt, who recorded the position of the comet on eight occasions between 13 and 23 August. Its presence near the bright star Arcturus helped Apian measure its position with a special instrument he had invented called a 'Meteoroscope' – devised for making graphic and rapid calculations in spherical astronomy. A consequence of these observations was that Apian proved that comet tails usually point away from the Sun *(see Fig. 7, p. 77)*.

The 1456 apparition, which Halley had suspected but not proved, was left to Pingré to convert to certainty. At this apparition the comet was described by historians of the day as 'great, terrible and of an extraordinary magnitude' and 'training after, its tail spread across two celestial signs [or 60°]'.

The nucleus of the comet was reported sometimes to have shone like a bright star, and the tail is described in one account as of a brilliant golden colour (attributable in the modern understanding of comets to sodium emissions in the head).

In 1456 the Turks under Mahomet II were confronting the Papal forces. Both armies regarded the comet as an omen of defeat and divine displeasure. Hunniades was defending Belgrade, and so great was the terror of the comet and the Turks that Callistus III ordered public prayers to be offered up for the deliverance from the comet and the enemies of Christendom. One story relates the Pope actually excommunicated the comet, but this version has been shown to be an eighteenth-century hoax – a tale put about by a French author out of humour with the Church – now thoroughly dismissed.[1]

Working backwards from 1456, Halley had also tried to extend recognition of the comet to 1380 and then 1305. But here he came unstuck and made errors of two and four years respectively. The actual years were later found to be 1378 and 1301. Others following Halley also attempted similar correlations. In April 1835, when the resighting of the comet was keenly anticipated, an article appeared in the *Edinburgh Review* written by an author who wished to distinguish himself in historical scholarship. Primed with the (incomplete) knowledge that Halley's comet came round every 75/76 years, he looked through a catalogue of previous comet sightings and, applying the necessary chronological yardstick, ticked off bright comets that had appeared at these intervals . . . Hey presto! Nothing could be simpler; he obtained dates for previous appearances of Halley's comet in 1456, 1380, 1305, 1230, 1005, 930, 550, 399, 323 and 130 BC. We now know all but the first date – which Halley had already suspected anyway – are wrong; this would-be scholar was blissfully unaware that owing to planetary perturbations, the passage of Halley's comet round the Sun may vary several years from a median of 75/76 years.

In the light of more modern records the shortest period known with certainty is 74 years 5½ months, between 1835 and 1910, while the longest is 79 years 5 months, between AD 451 and 530. To arrive at sure dates for apparitions previous to 1456 required some remarkable historical scholarship in the hands of several men.

The first to play historical detective after Pingré was the French computer Burckhardt, who investigated the orbit of a comet observed in China in 989. This comet is also mentioned in several Anglo-Saxon chronicles. He later proved it was Halley's comet. Three other appearances were identified by Laugier, of the Paris Observatory, who, using Chinese records, was able to identify its apparition in AD 451 when its reappearance coincided with the Battle of Châlons where the Roman general Aëtius defeated Attila. At this time European records which describe the comet are almost useless for scientific purposes. All one reads about in European accounts are astrological babblings while those of the Chinese star-clerks are cool narratives, accurate enough to pinpoint the comet's path in AD 451 through the Pleiades into Leo and Virgo and to set the perihelion passage for 3 July that year. Laugier was also to correct Halley's date of 1380 to 1378 and to identify another apparition in 760. In 1846 he published his findings in *Comptus Rendus*.

By far the most exhaustive study before the twentieth century was that undertaken by the English astronomer John Russell Hind. Almost uniquely, Hind was a skilled observer as well as a brilliant computer. He discovered three comets and ten asteroids and later became superintendent of the British *Nautical Almanac*. In the comprehensive paper he published in the *Monthly Notices* of the Royal Astronomical Society in 1850, he brought the comet firmly back into the province of British astronomy from which it had languished since the death of Halley.

In his paper, Hind claimed to have identified sixteen previous returns of the comet. Four of these were subsequently called into question by later researchers, and this is indicative of the difficulty inherent in fixing sure past dates. The remaining twelve, however, have all been vindicated. Hind only failed with the four in question because even the Chinese observations he relied upon were sometimes unclear or insufficient in number to establish the orbit with the necessary precision. His most noteworthy identification was the apparition in April 1066 when the Normans invaded England and King Harold's forces were routed. The comet was fortunately also recorded in the Chinese annals, and it was from these Hind was able to compute its orbit and identify it with the famous comet depicted on the Bayeux Tapestry.

Chinese observers first saw the comet on 2 April 1066, and Japanese astronomers independently the following morning. At this time the comet was located in Pegasus and was reported to have a thin tail pointing southwest and extending across the constellation into nearby Aquarius. Apart from the evidence of the comet on the Bayeux Tapestry itself, only a few European observations of this particular comet have subsequently come to light. The most reliable one was found in 1910 in the archives of the cathedral at Viterbo in Italy which records: 'In the year 1066 from the incarnation of the Lord, on 5th April a comet appeared in the East, and shone for 15 days, that is until the 19th, and the same appeared in the West in the evening on the 24th, like the eclipsed Moon, the tail of which steamed like smoke up to nearly half of the sky, and it shone until nearly the beginning of June.'

The *Anglo Saxon Chronicle* records it as follows: '. . . In this year King Harold came from York to Westminster at Easter, which was after the mid winter in which the King [Edward the Confessor] died. Then was seen over all England such a sign in the heavens as no man ever before saw; some say it was the star Cometa, which some men call the haired star; and it first appeared on the eve of Litani-major, the 8th of the Kalends of May [24 April], and so shone all the seven nights.'

According to the proverb of the time, a new 'star' meant a new sovereign, and in England prayers were said to have been offered throughout the kingdom to forestall the disastrous portent. William of Malmesbury, reporting several generations after the event, told of 'a certain monk of our monastery [Malmesbury Abbey] named Elmer, who bowing down with terror at the sight of the brilliant star exclaimed: "Here art thou again, cause of tears to many mothers. It is a long time since I saw thee last, but I see thee now, more terrible than ever, thou threatenest my country with utter ruin" '.

It is doubtful if Elmer had seen the earlier apparition in 989. It is possible, of course, as a number of people in history record two sightings in their lifetimes. Mark Twain saw it in 1835 and then again from his death-bed in April 1910. Lewis Swift, a doyen among nineteenth-century American comet hunters, also lived during both these apparitions, but by 1910 his wonderful eyesight had failed him. If Elmer had indeed seen a comet earlier, it was probably the bright comet of 1006, reported in Europe and in China, or probably another comet of which there are several round this period, at present uncatalogued because their true paths are unknown.

An apparition of Halley's comet recognized by Hind was that of 1301 when it was observed in Europe and China. This apparition is supposedly recounted in Giotto's painting, the Adoration of the Magi where the comet is seen as a direct representation of the Star of Bethlehem. Two other apparitions also recognized by Hind were 11-12 BC and AD 66. Over the years much speculation has involved these two apparitions as the possible source for the story of the Star of Bethlehem seen at the time of the birth of Christ. At the 11-12 BC appearance, the earliest recorded by Hind, the comet is reported to have terrified the Romans before the death of Agrippa. Likewise, next time round in AD 66, it terrified the Jews when they were hard pressed by the Romans at the siege of Jerusalem when Josephus records that several prodigies announced the destruction of the city and there was 'Amongst other warnings, a comet, of the kind called Xiphias, because their tails appear to represent the blade of a sword'. It was also at this return the comet is alleged to have been seen by St Peter, just before his martyrdom.

The finest early depiction of the comet is the AD 684 apparition which appears in the *Nuremberg Chronicle*, and this physically resembles a comet much more than the stylized 'logo' object later woven into the Bayeux Tapestry.

Note

[1] The hoary chestnut about the Pope's excommunication of Halley's comet in 1456 crops up repeatedly in both popular and serious literature. It was thoroughly dismissed by W.T. Lynn in *Notes & Queries* 7th Series, i, 471; and 9th Series, ii, 517. A complete discussion was also published by Father Stein in No II (1909) of the publications of the Specola Vaticana.

8 · A Coronation Comet – 1909-11

N THE DECADES subsequent to the fading of Halley's comet in May 1836, the world was treated to some spectacular visitations of a number of bright comets. The first of these was in 1843 when a new, super-brilliant comet was seen only 4° distant from the Sun's edge. Later, after it passed into the night sky, it developed a tail over 70° long.

The 1843 comet proved only the forerunner of other bright comets later to be called Sungrazers, so named owing to their very close approaches to the Sun – actually skimming through the Sun's atmosphere. Bright Sungrazers appeared in January 1880, May 1882, September 1882 and January 1887.[1]

The Sungrazer of September 1882 was a particularly noteworthy object, and its nucleus was seen to divide into at least four distinct parts and give birth to several independent comets. Another comet seen to divide was Biela's comet in 1846. On its return in 1852 it greeted astronomers with the unusual spectacle of one principal comet accompanied by a satellite comet now separated by a distance of 2.4 million km. However, on subsequent scheduled returns neither comet has been seen again.[2]

Another spectacular comet of the nineteenth century was Donati's comet of 1858. In September-October that year it hung in the night sky like a scimitar and passed over the bright star Arcturus. The various contemporary portrayals of the comet show three well-defined tails: two narrow, straight ones, which in the light of today's knowledge we can interpret as gas (plasma) tails, and a very conspicuous, broad scimitar-shaped tail composed of fine dust particles.

Donati's comet was the first ever successfully photographed, but it was not until 1882 after the introduction of dry plates that the brilliant comet of September that year was captured in its full glory.

From here on it was appreciated that comet photography was a powerful tool in the hands of astronomers. With improving photographic techniques a plate exposed to record a comet could capture a wealth of fine detail, particularly in the tail, and reveal details not directly visible to the human eye even with the largest telescopes. Photographs taken from hour to hour and night to night provided a permanent record of the rapidly changing structures in the head and tail, with the added advantage they could be measured and studied at more leisure from the comfort of an office desk during daylight hours. Equally important, positions of comets could be measured with great accuracy.

The first comet actually discovered by photography was quite by accident when a plate exposed on 17 May 1882 to record the total eclipse of the Sun in Egypt showed the presence of a previously unseen

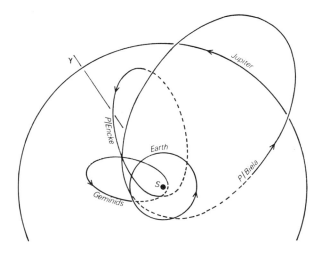

Fig. 9   The orbits of Biela's and Encke's comets and that occupied by the Geminid meteors. The Geminids have no known association with a now recognized comet. However, in 1983 a tiny Earth-crossing Apollo asteroid, or minor planet, designated 1983 TB, was discovered to occupy approximately this orbit. Whether this is simply coincidence or whether 1983 TB represents a class of 'asteroidal' body associated with comets and meteors remains uncertain.

Sungrazing comet. Another accidental discovery made in similar fashion was during a solar eclipse on 16 April 1893. Since then several other comets have been recorded during eclipses. The first man to pioneer photography as a regular method of comet hunting was the American E.E. Barnard in October 1892. Before this Barnard had discovered a number of comets by the traditional visual method. The photographic method soon proved superior, although it has never entirely superseded the older method still used today by amateur comet hunters.

But photography was not the only new technique applied to comets. The spectroscope devised by early nineteenth-century physicists to analyse the chemical nature of a light source was first applied to comets in 1864 when the unmistakable presence of carbon was detected. The spectroscope also revealed that comets as a class of body not only shine by reflected light (from the Sun) as discovered earlier by Arago (p. 104) but they also emit light due to excitation in the comet's head, triggered off by the stimulus of sunlight. However, deciphering the chemistry of comets unambiguously has proved a difficult task, and even today definitive answers are lacking.

*　　　　*　　　　*

As the nineteenth century closed and the twentieth dawned, the return of Halley's comet was not far from everyone's mind. Since the comet had retreated in 1836, many brilliant and interesting comets had come and then faded into oblivion. With the new tool of photography, the number of comets discovered annually multiplied several fold.

Just prior to the reappearance of Halley's comet, a new comet was discovered photographically by Morehouse at Des Moines University Observatory, USA, on 1 September 1908. It was then only a faint, insignificant 9^m object, but later it developed into one of the most unusual ever seen.

During the course of its apparition the comet travelled from pole to pole. It remained in the northern skies for several weeks and became a prime photographic subject. The spectrum of Morehouse's comet now revealed for the first time the presence of poisonous cyanogen gas, hitherto unrecognized in comets. Clearly comets were very strange bodies, and with each advance in technology they were becoming even stranger.

*　　　　*　　　　*

Flushed with his success in predicting the return of Halley's comet to within four days in 1835, Pontecoulant had extended his calculations to the next return and had already published them forty-six years before the comet was to make its twentieth-century debut. According to the Frenchman the comet would come back to perihelion during April 1910.

It was known that between 1835 and 1910 the comet would undergo great perturbations by Jupiter, especially in the earlier part of this interval. The question was: by how much?

Around the time Pontecoulant made his forecast, the Swedish astronomer Anders Jonas Angström also looked into the question and, following Hind's identifications, predicted the comet would in fact return some time during or even after 1912.

In the early years of the century, two British professionals working at Greenwich declared their interest in the comet and, assisted by three volunteer helpers, set out on the time-consuming task of attempting to forecast the perihelion time as precisely as humanly possible. With Hind's researches into its past appearances, the comet had come back into the care of Halley's own countrymen. Now the five-man British team (one was an Irishman) were not going to let it escape again into the hands of the old rivals across the Channel.

Heading the quintet of computers were P.H. Cowell and the Irishman A.C.D. Crommelin; their assistants were W.M. Smart, F.R. Cripps and T. Wright. All were civil servants at Greenwich Observatory where Halley had reigned as incumbent Astronomer Royal for twenty-two years. The task before them was formidable. Using Hind's list as a basis, their plan was to go back to first principles and endeavour to retrace the comet step by step to each previous apparition, making sure that at every return it was positively identified before proceeding back in time to the next earliest one.

By now comets had been recognized as very flimsy bodies; while sometimes voluminous, they, nevertheless, had little mass in comparison with the planets or their satellites. In 1868 a comet was known to have passed very close to Jupiter and then to have wandered right through its system of satellites. Although the comet itself was thrown into an entirely new orbit, the encounter did not affect the planet nor its statellites in any way which could be measured.

In computing any comet's future orbit, account needs to be taken of all the different perturbations a comet may be subjected to during its wanderings in the solar system. In the case of Halley's comet its movements are chiefly determined by the Sun's attraction alone, but there are occasions when its presence near Jupiter, or one of the other large planets, creates a significant third force as Halley and Newton had first realized back in the seventeenth century.

118

In the period 1836-1910 it was known that this time round the revolution interval would be shortened, and its quick return, paradoxically, would be due to *delays* caused by Jupiter.

The orbits of Halley's comet and Jupiter cross approximately at two points, and the time occupied by the planet in moving from one to the other in its orbit is nearly equal to that occupied by the comet in its orbit. As a consequence, if both are near one crossing-point together, they will also be near the other point together.

During the interval 1836-1910, Jupiter got behind the comet on both these occasions and pulled it back – the direct effect of which is *delay*. However, an indirect effect overpowers this. The comet does not travel as far afield when it is checked in its path at the outset and therefore as a result comes back to the Sun *more quickly*. At its limit, Halley's comet

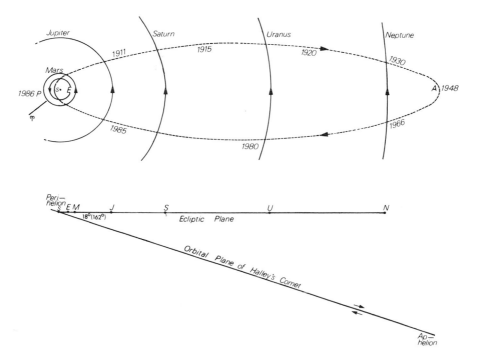

Fig. 10   The orbit of Halley's comet. The dates indicate the various positions of the comet during its last revolution round the Sun 1910-86. Unlike the major planets whose orbits lie in one plane (the ecliptic), many comets have paths which are inclined. Unlike the planets, some comets go round the Sun clockwise (or retrograde), and Halley's comet is one example of this type.

journeys out to the boundaries of the solar system far beyond the orbit of Neptune to a distance of 4,800 million km. The peculiarity of its elliptic motion, under the gravity of the Sun, is that it spends half its revolution time dawdling in the small arc beyond Neptune's orbit. This is a consequence of Kepler's third law, viz, equal areas in equal times. While it spends *years* out at this part of its orbit, it only spends *weeks* in the inner, opposite arc as it rounds the Sun (Fig. 10). At its remotest from the Sun, the lingering part of the comet's journey becomes accentuated as the time of revolution increases.

For the 1910 apparition the Greenwich team decided to apply to the comet a new mathematical technique developed a little earlier by Cowell to investigate the orbit of Jupiter's tiny eighth satellite. It had proved very successful and allowed this very faint body to be resighted by observers.

Before any ephemeris could be computed for the new apparition of Halley's comet, the team first faced the laborious task of backtracking the comet through history.

In spite of the past researches of Pingré, Burckhardt, Laugier and Hind, plus other work by some oriental scholars, several previous identifications were still uncertain. The observations contained in the Chinese annals were indispensable for this work. Hind had identified the comet in old records by utilizing descriptions and then tracing out the observed paths across the constellations, but some of the information to hand was often vague and at best uncertain. In contrast, the modus operandi adopted by Cowell and Crommelin was to concentrate on accurate calculations of the lengths of successive revolutions round the Sun as the comet was affected by perturbations. Hind had identified Halley's comet as a comet that had appeared in 1223 which chroniclers cited as being the instrument and precursor of the death of the French king, Philip Augustus. After due deliberation, Cowell and Crommelin discarded this comet and gave preference to another seen in August and September the previous year in 1222 that probably was at perihelion in September. Chinese annals record it as having a tail '31 cubits long' and noted it 'perished in two months'.

Cowell and Crommelin also looked again at Hind's identification of AD 912. There were probably two comets that year. While Hind chose one visible in May, the Greenwich pair preferred one seen in August.

Halley's comet should also have appeared in AD 837. European and Chinese accounts again imply two bright comets that year, and it is possible there were three or even four. Cowell and Crommelin chose one that was at perihelion at the end of February or beginning of March. It is

120

now known that on 9 April 837, Halley's comet approached the Earth to within 6 million km and in a single day traversed over 60° of sky. Chinese records report a tail of '80 feet', equal in modern terms to more than 100°. The comet must have presented a dramatic and frightening sight, and it is not surprising the ancients went in terror of it. Except for 1910, its tail then was the longest ever seen visually on any comet before or since.

Hind had chosen a comet which had appeared in AD 608. This comet had been observed by the Chinese when it passed over the constellations Auriga, Ursa Major and Scorpius. Cowell and Crommelin rejected this and preferred a comet seen the previous year in 607.

When the Greenwich team arrived at Hind's identification of 11 BC and duly confirmed it, they then moved back into terra incognita. The history of the comet was now uncertain, but using the Chinese records as a guide, they identified the comet's orbital fingerprints in turn back to 87 BC, 163 BC and 240 BC

This is where Cowell and Crommelin called a halt; beyond this date-line the sightings were too conjectural. They were aware, of course, that Pingré in his *Cométographie* made references to comets in remote antiquity. However, the earliest that seemed to rest on reliable evidence was a comet seen in China in 611 BC. Cowell and Crommelin believed it possible that this might have been Halley's comet, but its sure identity was wanting. Yet another apparition was perhaps that of 467 BC seen in Europe and China and this is perhaps the same comet mentioned by Aristotle in his book *Meteor*.

On 28 July 1908, Crommelin wrote to his friend the astronomer H.H. Turner, the Savilian Professor of Astronomy at Oxford: 'We have now carried back Halley's comet to BC 87 (August) with certainty (one revolution earlier than Hind's list), and with fair probability to BC 240 (May). Hind is one-and-a-half years too late for his 608 AD return (it really was 607 March), but all his earlier returns are right up to the beginning of his list (– 11 = BC 12). We find 12.9 April 1910 for the next passage, but we are going over the work again by a new method.'

Subsequently, Cowell and Crommelin put back the perihelion date to 16.61 April 1910 *(See Table p. 180)*.

As with the previous apparitions in 1758-9 and 1835-6, special efforts were mounted to detect the comet as early as possible. This time, however, there was a big difference from former times. The new tool of photography was available and, since the pioneer comet pictures of the 1880s, there had been rapid technical advances. No one among the professional ranks now dreamed of wasting long hours glued to the eyepiece of a telescope sweeping the skies when the guided time-exposed photographic plate could penetrate much farther into space and then after development be examined in comfort the next day.

The first photograph known to have been taken to try to catch the comet was made by O.J. Lee at the Yerkes Observatory, Chicago, on 22 December 1908. Also in the race early were the staff at the Royal Greenwich Observatory, keen to back up their computer colleagues as often as the all-prevailing cloud and smogs of London would allow them to observe.

It was thought a unique opportunity to see the comet early would be offered during the total eclipse of the Sun in Tasmania on 8 May 1909; then, disappointingly, it was realized the comet would have set below the horizon before the eclipse began.

As the summer of 1909 approached and then passed, observers became anxious. It was the middle of September before word was telegraphed round the world that the comet had at last been resighted by 'Wolf of Heidelberg'.

Maximilian (Max) Wolf, Director of the Königstuhl Observatory, was a past-master at the art of celestial photography. Earlier, on 27 December 1891, he had detected his first asteroid using the pioneer trail method. Now, on a plate he had exposed on 11 September 1909, near the star Gamma Gemini, he could just pick out the minute image of the returning comet, not more than 10' of arc from the position predicted by the British team. At this time the comet lay at a distance of 512 million km from the Earth.

After the first announcements, other observers searched their earlier plates. Unbeknowingly the Royal Greenwich Observatory had recorded it on 9 September, but its photographic image went undetected. Thus the prize slipped from their grasp. At Helwan Observatory, in the transparent skies of Egypt, the minute image of the comet had impressed itself as early as 24 August. Even Wolf now discovered he had overlooked an earlier image of 28 August.

After the resighting, some quick computations revealed the actual perihelion passage would be 19.64 April 1910 (later corrected to 20.18 April 1910) – or within about three days of Cowell's and Crommelin's second, more accurate, prediction of 16.6 April 1910. In some respects this was a disappointing result for the British computers after the effort expended. Nevertheless, it was a much closer prediction than any other. The Lindemann Prize of 1,000 marks which had been offered by the

Astronomische Gesellschaft for the most successful prediction was now awarded to Cowell and Crommelin.

The 3.03-day discrepancy puzzled Cowell and Crommelin; it convinced them there were other unknown (non-gravitational) forces at work on the comet. On 5 March 1910 they wrote: 'It now appears from observation that the predicted time of 16.61 April is 3.03 [3.58] days too early. At least two days of this error must be attributed to causes other than errors in calculation or errors in the adopted position and masses of the planets.'

Crommelin's personal copy of their winning Essay which he received and annotated with his name on 11 April 1910 is now a prized possession of the author. Later annotations by Crommelin on its inside pages indicate that years after he was still having ideas how their predictions might yet be improved to match the actual perihelion time more closely.

*   *   *

After the reappearance of Halley's comet had been announced in the autumn of 1909, telescopes, large and small, were trained onto the rare visitor. First visual sighting, as opposed to an image on a photographic plate, was reported on 15 September 1909 by the eagle-eyed American, double-star observer, S.W. Burnham, using the 101-cm Yerkes Observatory refractor then, and still, the largest telescope of its type in the world.

Barnard, a colleague of Burnham, saw it visually through the same telescope two nights later on the 17th. These two astronomers were often great rivals for 'firsts' and often frustrated by the other's use of the great telescope as the observing-time was shared and rostered to a strict schedule. Certainly on this occasion Barnard, primarily a comet man, was piqued at being beaten by Burnham, a double-star observer.

During September, and through the remaining months of 1909, the comet gradually brightened as it approached the Sun. On 19 October, Barnard estimated it was 13^m. By November it was 12^m, then in the middle of the month a rudimentary tail was first detected. By late November it was 10.5^m, and one observer reported fluctuations in brightness.

By January 1910 the comet was getting brighter by the day. Then overnight, when all interest was centred on Halley's comet, a much more brilliant unannounced interloper suddenly breezed in from the wings and for several days stole the headlines.

This unexpected comet first showed itself in the southern hemisphere in the dawn skies of 12 January when diamond miners and railway workers in South Africa independently noticed it as they travelled home after working nightshift. Some days later, on the 17th, it was an even more spectacular object and could be seen in full daylight just 4° from the Sun. Towards the end of January the tail had grown to a length of 40°, and the comet had moved north. It was now a distinct yellowish tinge owing to sodium emissions triggered by its close approach to the Sun. At its brightest it outshone Venus, but the display was soon over. By middle February the comet had sunk below naked-eye visibility and was only a moderate telescopic object. It continued to fade and by 9 July was at the limit of visibility.

During January it had been seen in the tropics as a truly brilliant daylight comet; even in northern Europe it was a twilight one. To the public and the media the sudden appearance of another comet created utter confusion and provided a celestial comedy of errors. Previously all talk was centred on Halley's comet. Then fate intervened, and a garbled telegraphic message from South Africa hummed over the wires with the story of the discovery of 'Drake's comet' (instead of a 'great comet'). Some newspapers next morning were full of 'Drake's comet'. Who was this mysterious Drake? Halley, yes, the informed public and newspaper men vaguely knew about him as the Englishman who had predicted an early return of the comet now fast approaching the Sun . . . but Drake? Yet on second thoughts there was *a* Drake, an historical figure much better known than Halley, for had not Sir Francis Drake helped destroy the Armada! The problem now was that resourceful newspapermen could not find any record of Sir Francis ever having dabbled in astronomy let alone discovered a comet.

Through late January the media could not quite agree among themselves what to call this apparition out of the blue. 'Drake's comet' remained a firm favourite until others decided 'Halley's comet' was a safer bet. Some journalists queried whether perhaps even the astronomers themselves were confused. In the end it became the 'Daylight comet', or the 'Miners' comet', but as it faded, its advent turned into a seven-day press wonder.

*   *   *

During January 1910, astronomers had been watching both comets. By the end of January, Halley's comet had brightened to 9^m3; in February it was 8^m, and the tail was 40' long. The head was now showing a system of rays, and small jets were seen emerging from the nuclear region in a way reminiscent of the 1835-6 apparition, except now they were repeated on a smaller scale.

By the beginning of February it was plainly visible in small amateur telescopes, shining like a small nebula. On 9 February, Wolf claimed, after seeing it through theatre glasses, also to have glimpsed it with the naked eye and described it as 'easily visible'. Several observers were now reporting a multiple nucleus.

In early March it was still officially around 8^m, and photographs plainly showed the tail and the numerous ray structures, and jets emerging from the head.

In the latter part of March, as it neared the Sun, it passed out of the night sky and did not reappear until the middle of April. When it reappeared, the comet was close to perihelion and had brightened to 2^{m}5. Photographs taken at this time show parabolic envelopes of fine tenuous matter and some denser concentrations in the head.

By early May the tail was 6° long and divided. By 17 May the tail had lengthened enormously, but cited estimates at this time vary and are conflicting. Some observers traced out the tail to over 70° and estimated its breadth as 9°.

In the tropics especially, the comet was a glorious early-morning spectacle. It was now close to Venus, and this pair of brilliant objects in near conjunction presented a rare sight, stirring even the lethargic from their beds to witness it. By 1910, astronomers, like other scientists, had slipped into the habit of using the flat unemotional jargon of their trade. In hundreds of reports of Halley's comet we can read about precise measurements of the coma, magnitude, length of tail in degrees, etc, but few let themselves go with purple passages as their less inhibited predecessors once did. Verbal, descriptive observations were now frowned upon as old-fashioned and most 'unscientific'. In contrast, others had no such inhibitions. On 18 May a London correspondent based in Accra, West Africa, wrote home: '. . . Here everyone has gone mad over it, and we all get up at 4 am, and sit and gaze at it till it gets light. It is *the* most wonderful thing ever seen. The comet itself rises far above the horizon, but its tail which stands straight up, is like the rays of a very powerful search-light – so long, that it reaches from the horizon to the very roof of the heavens; and so broad that it occupies roughly one fourth of the arc of the sky; and its light is so powerful that combined with Venus (which is also lovely just now), it has almost the effect of a midnight Sun. The

125

natives are frightened to death of it, and will have it that it means an earthquake coming . . .'

Elsewhere cranks were predicting the end of the world, and the credulous stared in horror of it much like their medieval forebears once did. In the American West, itinerant patent medicine vendors were doing a brisk trade selling comet pills to ward off its evil influence and cashing in on the heaven-sent opportunity to fleece an ever gullible public. In February 1910 a neurotic in Valencia, Spain, became obsessed with the idea the comet would collide with the Earth and plunged to his death from a bedroom window, killing himself instantly. It was shades of Lalande and the Paris doom-watchers of 1772 . . . Then when King Edward VII suddenly died in London on 6 May 1910, there were those who in hindsight recognized Halley's comet in the vein of the old Anglo-Saxon proverb of 1066 when a new 'star' signified a coronation in the offing.[3]

By the middle of May 1910, as the London correspondent in Accra had noted, the tail had lengthened enomously. On 18 May the comet's orbit carried it between the Earth and the Sun. Because of this unique event, an American expedition was speedily sent to Hawaii to observe the Sun's disc

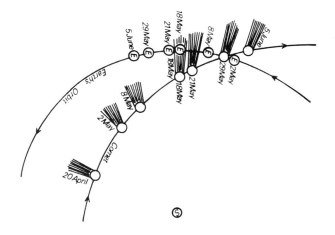

Fig. 11   In May 1910 the Earth passed through the tail of Halley's comet. The Earth and the comet were nearest to each other on 18 May, but since the dust tail curved backwards, passage through it was slightly delayed. From the direction of the Earth the head of the comet transitted the Sun, but nothing of the nucleus was observed against the bright disk.

126

at the critical time; but not a trace of the comet's nucleus projected on the background of the Sun's disc was seen. From these observations it was concluded that had there been a solid body 320km in diameter forming a nucleus to the comet, it would have been readily spotted.

On 19 May, 75° of tail was visible above the horizon and 30° below so that it reached a total length of 105°, even surpassing the tail-length reported by the Chinese in the AD 837 apparition. As also in AD 837 the comet was now close to the Earth. On 20-21 May, when the Earth was due to pass through the tail, a special look-out was kept to note any peculiar atmospheric or meteorological phenomena which might be attributed to the comet. However, the Earth only passed through the outer edge of the tail and at its closest was at least 8 million km distant from the comet's head (*Fig. 11*). Owing to brilliant moonlight, no positive atmospheric effects were confirmed; but, as expected, because of the wide publicity afforded the event by the world's press, there were hundreds of eye-witness reports of alleged unusual happenings in the sky.

At 2.30 am on 19 May a soft glow could be seen diffusing from below Cassiopeia. A few hours later, tail streamers from the comet were distinctly visible in spite of strong moonlight, and the 'train' of the comet stretched across the sky for at least 140°. By the end of May it was still a 2^m object, but the brilliant display was now coming to an end. As the comet gradually drew away from the Sun, it faded rapidly. At the beginning of June it had dimmed to 3^m5; in July 5^m5, and by the end of the month 7^m0.

On 12 November 1910, now well on course towards its aphelion beyond Neptune, Barnard estimated the comet's brightness as 11^m. In April 1911 it was still in view, and at the end of the month, Barnard was reporting it to be of variable brightness and shining around 14^m5 to 15^m, The last view of it visually was on 29 April at the Helwan Observatory, and the same observatory followed it photographically until June 1911 by which time it had receded from the Sun to a distance of 837 million km, well beyond the orbit of Jupiter.

Notes

[1] The so-called Sungrazer comets form a remarkable group of objects. In 1888 the German astronomer Kreutz was among the first to draw attention to the curious similarity of the orbits of several comets including the great comet of 1843 and the spate of Sungrazers in the 1880s. Nowadays these and later examples of the Sungrazer genre are often referred to as the Kreutz group.

The Sungrazers are not as infrequent as once thought. In 1982 a team working at the Naval Research Laboratory in Washington DC, using a satellite observatory, detected several new members. All these were unobserved from Earth, but all were smaller bodies than the great Sungrazers observed in the past. One of these, comet Howard-Koomen-Michels 1979 XI, was seen to collide with the Sun on 31 August 1979 and then throw up a cloud of debris. The two later ones encountered the Sun on 27 January 1981 and 20 July 1981 respectively and neither comet reappeared. These observations tend to confirm that small Sungrazers of this type may be expected to encounter the Sun at a frequency of one every six months. The number of those observed also lends support to the theory that perhaps all Sungrazers belonged in the past to one great parent comet which divided and then subdivided into many parts because of the disrupting tidal forces of the Sun. (*See also note 3, chapter 9*).

[2] Biela's comet is associated with the spectacular meteor shower witnessed in late November 1872 when all over Europe 'shooting stars' came too fast to be counted. At least 50,000, perhaps 100,000, were seen by a single party of observers.

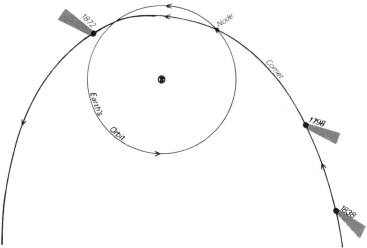

Fig. 12   The orbit of Biela's comet in relation to the Earth. Illustrated are the positions of the comet along its orbit when meteor showers occurred on the Earth in 1798 and 1838; this indicates that cosmic debris which entered the Earth's atmosphere, near the comet's node point, then lay in front of the comet (see also note 14).

In some books the impression given is that this display was proof of the final disintegration of Biela's comet. However, there is evidence of a shower of meteors having been seen from this same radiant back in AD 524, and there were brilliant displays in 1741, 1798, 1830 and 1838. There seems no doubt that meteors generally are very closely related to comets and probably represent cometary debris, for there are many instances where they occupy the same orbit; nevertheless, their precise interrelationship is still not absolutely clear. In 1798, 1830 and 1838 the meteors occupying Biela's orbit originated from a point *in front* of the (known) Biela comets. (*Fig. 12*).

It is possible that the lost Biela comet(s) may one day be resighted as other 'lost' comets have been successfully recovered. The problem is the orbit of Biela's comet is subject to marked changes; as a result of this the main meteor stream no longer intersects the Earth's orbit as favourably as it did in the past.

The search for the lost comet, or a remnant, continues. It is of interest that the bright comet 1973f (*see p. 135*) was found accidentally by Luboš Kohoutek during one such abortive photographic search.

³ A Victorian-age comet scare occurred in 1857 when it was predicted a great comet seen in 1264, with a tail 100° in length and curved like a sabre, would make its return. It was a comet which astrologers had blamed for the death of Pope Urban IV.

The same comet had supposedly been seen again in 1556 when it was not nearly so conspicuous as formerly. Halley was particularly interested in this comet when he investigated the past orbits of comets for his *Synopsis* (*Table 1*). He concluded the comet of 1264 and 1556 were identical, and its period therefore was about 292 years. He predicted it would reappear about 1848 . . .

Others after Halley investigated its orbit including Pingré who concurred with his predecessor's findings. John Russell Hind also took an interest and, after correcting some obvious errors in Pingré's computations, derived an orbit as did a Dutchman named Bomme. After reckoning perturbations by the planets, a new period was computed and a prediction made that the comet would reach perihelion on 2 August 1858. However, in spite of this, there was still some uncertainty of about two years in the date.

Much publicity was engendered among the lay public. A really bright comet had not been seen since 1843. A German astrologer predicted it would collide with the Earth, and a Belgian almanac-maker provided the exact date of 13 June. The new celestial threat was expected to be the sight of a lifetime. Although there were many scoffers about this prediction, the anticipated event gave rise to a plethora of sensational literature – just as Kohoutek's comet did in 1973-4. A typical example was a sixpenny pamphlet, now a prized possession of the author, entitled *Will The Great Comet now Rapidly Approaching Strike The Earth?* It was written in a highly charged pseudo-scientific style by a James Bedford PhD, and among advice the author offered his lay readership – ever conscious of cholera and fevers – was '. . . to keep all kinds of refuse and filth a distance from the dwellings as they would at times of plague; to look well to drainage; to keep no old left off or unused clothes of any kind in holes and corners . . .'

To the relief of the ignorant but alas for the confidence of Halley, Pingré, Hind and Bomme . . . the long-suspected comet never materialized. Fortunately, to let the astronomers off the hook, Donati's totally unexpected comet filled the night skies the following year, and many of the general public were none the wiser. In hindsight, Halley's record for comet prediction was a poor one. He was wrong about the comet of 1680/1, the comets of 1532/1661, and now the comets of 1264/1556. It is fortunate his reputation had already been made by the return of the 1682 comet in 1758 otherwise history might now be remembering him as a sometime amanuensis of Newton who never quite made the grade.

9 · Comets and the Space Age

THE 1909-11 APPARITION of Halley's comet had been the first opportunity to examine it critically using the spectroscope in hope of deciphering its chemical make-up. By now astronomers specializing in physical studies of celestial bodies were called astrophysicists. Since the pioneer studies of the late 1850s and early 1860s, the science of spectroscopy had made some noteworthy advances, particularly in the study of the nature of stars. However, in their studies of comets, astrophysicists were still frustrated. There were tentative clues about the various solids and gases that make up comets, but knowledge about them was very sketchy. Back in 1882 two astronomers claimed to have observed the emission spectra of calcium and several metals in the head of the Sungrazer comet of 1882 (II) near the time of its perihelion. While some accepted these observations at face value, others believed mistakes had been made in interpretation. As they were only visual observations and could not be rechecked (photo-spectroscopy for comets was still years away), their reality was doubted for many generations. They were not vindicated until over eighty years later when the same emission-lines were recognized in the spectacular Ikeya-Seki Sungrazer of 1965.

A sure constituent identified in comets was sodium which often signals its presence by tingeing the comet with a yellowish hue near time of perihelion. Throughout history many 'yellow' or 'golden' comets have

131

been reported, and no doubt this colour was a genuine manifestation as opposed to some other bizarre colours cited by ancient chroniclers.[1]

During the 1909-11 apparition the tail, as well as the head, of Halley's comet was also studied intensively. What now became certain was that comet tails were composed of very fine tenuous material. In 1910, K. Schwarzschild estimated that if the tail of Halley's comet at its greatest length were composed of only fine dust particles, it might weigh possibly 1 million tonnes, but if it were only tenuous gas, not more than 1,000 tonnes. A gas tail of this type is much less dense than the Earth's atmospheric envelope, therefore no effects would be noted when the Earth passed through it, as occurred in May 1910.

The realization that a comet's tail was a very tenuous structure gave rise to the popular, if slightly disparaging, modern description that a comet is nothing more than 'a great big bag full of nothing'. While this is a tongue-in-cheek exaggeration, it, nevertheless, contains an element of truth, and discoveries in the late 1960s and '70s were to confirm the idea. By the first decades of the twentieth century it was clear that apart from the 'solid' nucleus of a comet, of which absolutely nothing was known, comets as cosmic bodies were lightweights. Indeed the density of a typical comet envelope (excluding the nucleus) might be appreciated by imagining a volume of space measuring one cubic km with twelve small marbles spaced equidistantly inside it.

In William Herschel's time, astronomers of the eighteenth century had often posed the question: are comets habitable? Herschel himself believed they were . . . Noah Webster, the great lexicographer and famous for his *American Dictionary of the English Language*, was one among several scholars who was firmly of the opinion that influenza was introduced into the Earth's atmosphere by Halley's comet. Nineteenth-century astronomers laughed these ideas out of court, for now they knew better, and after the Earth had passed through the tail of the comet in May 1910, contemporary astronomers equally dismissed them as medieval nonsense. However, to the surprise of many, the question of life and germs in comets was raised again in the 1970s when Fred Hoyle and his colleague Chandra Wickramasinghe posed the challenge: do comets, in fact, provide travelling habitats for cosmic bacteria?

*   *   *

After Halley's comet retreated in 1911, there was a dearth of bright comets. One exception was Delavan's comet which for many months in

1914 became visible throughout the world and, not surprisingly, was singled out by the superstitious as the cosmic portender of World War I.

It was not until the middle 1950s, just before the Space Age, that any really bright comets came along in the northern hemisphere to match the now legendary ones of the nineteenth century; then two appeared within three months.[2] However, fainter, photographic, comets were being discovered in increasing numbers. It was not unusual for a dozen or more to be in view at any one time, yet most were dim objects and only visible in large telescopes.

In the 1960s one of the most noteworthy comets was the Ikeya-Seki Sungrazer seen in 1965. Half an hour before its closest approach to the Sun it broke up and separated into at least two distinct concentrations.[3]

It was now the Space Age, and more scientists observed the Ikeya-Seki comet than any previous to it. It had whetted the appetite of scientists who hitherto had ignored comets and sometimes dismissed them as relatively unimportant cosmic bodies in the solar system. Comets were now leading candidates for fly-by missions, using space probes, and plans were already afoot for a mission to Halley's comet in 1985-6.

A new interest in comets had begun slowly in the early 1950s after it was recognized that particle emission from the Sun interacting on a comet's head was a prime cause of some kinds of cometary tails. These particles from the Sun, known collectively as the solar wind, had been discovered to travel out from the Sun at speeds ranging from 1,000 to 2,000 km per second, plus a slower faction travelling at about 500 km per second. While similar ideas about the Sun's interaction with cometary heads had been put forward by Bessel in 1836, physical science then could not offer a convincing explanation how it occurred.

Because comets were found to be expecially sensitive to the newly discovered corpuscular radiation emanating from the Sun, astrophysicists began to use them as a kind of space 'barometer' by which the solar wind itself might be studied. It is the same corpuscular radiation from the Sun that can endanger astronauts in orbit round the Earth when the solar wind is sometimes blowing at storm force. And it is the same radiation that interacts with the Earth's magnetic field and produces brilliant displays of aurora in the upper atmosphere.

Following the recognition of the role of the solar wind on comets, comet tails were classified into two main types: tails consisting of ionized gases (or plasmas), and tails consisting of a variable mixture of dust and quasi-dust particles resulting from the more simple radiation pressure of sunlight.

Both types of tails are easily recognizable in photographs. The ionized gas tail is generally straight and narrow while the dust tail is strongly curved like a scimitar and tends to lag behind the line drawn between the comet and the Sun (the radius vector). The famous Donati comet of 1858 showed a magnificent tail-plume of what we now recognize to be 'dusty' material, but it also shows two narrower, almost straight, tails of ionized gases.

By the mid-sixties, radio astronomers were directing their large telescopes towards the comets in attempts to probe their physical make-up, but pioneer observations of the Ikeya-Seki Sungrazer to try to identify microwave radiation from the comet proved unsuccessful. Then an entirely new tool came to hand in the form of the Orbiting Astronomical Observatory 2 (OAO2), launched on 7 December 1968 . . .

The Earth's atmosphere acts as a shield, or filter, to certain radiations trying to enter it, and it had long been recognized that fundamental knowledge about the physical processes taking place inside a comet's head would likely never be forthcoming from Earth-bound observatories. If progress was to be made, the only solution was to place an observatory or laboratory outside the atmosphere. Until the era of artificial satellites this remained the pipe-dream of astronomers. By the late 1960s the old dream became reality . . .

The first comet to come under scrutiny was the earlier of two bright comets seen in 1969. This was discovered independently by a number of Japanese amateurs and later resolved itself in the catalogues under the title of comet Tago-Sato-Kosaka 1969 IX. The orbit of this comet proved to be very eccentric, and its period of revolution round the Sun is measured in some hundreds of thousands of years. Such an object, after visiting the Sun, would wander off into deep space, well beyond the farthest borders of the solar system, almost half-way towards the nearest stars before turning again for a rendezvous with the Sun. However, the most interesting fact about this comet, when observed from outside the Earth's atmosphere aboard OAO2, was the discovery of a vast cloud of tenuous hydrogen gas surrounding it, detected by the spacecraft's ultra-violet telescope.

The second comet of 1969 was discovered by the amateur John C. Bennett in South Africa on 28 December. During the early part of 1970 it slowly brightened as it travelled northwards in a path almost perpendicular to the Earth's orbit. It became a magnificant object in the morning skies towards the end of March and developed a resplendent 30° tail.

Bennett's comet was observed outside the atmosphere by the Orbiting Geophysical Observatory 5 (OGO5) when it was scanned in hydrogen-alpha light. Like its earlier cousin Tago-Sato-Kosaka it was found to be surrounded by a vast tenuous hydrogen cloud which was traced out to a distance of 13 million km in the direction parallel with the tail. Comets were now, indeed, proved to be mostly gas bags and even more flimsy than was thought at the beginning of the century.

The period from the middle 1960s to the middle 1970s was a truly vintage decade for bright comets – and the occasional damp squib. In the southern hemisphere especially, the astronomers and public alike had been treated to a series of spectaculars only known back in the nineteenth century. Then in 1973 there was the sudden promise of a comet which might perhaps outshine all those seen previously.

This new comet was discovered in March 1973 by the Czech astronomer Luboš Kohoutek. After its orbit was computed, it was predicted that, although not a Sungrazer, it might become a conspicuous object late the following December and in January 1974. If it lived up to the most optimistic expectations, it would be seen as the brightest comet apparition ever witnessed – surpassing some legendary comets reported in Greek and Roman times – and provide the celestial spectacle of the twentieth century.

It was now that the popular media, fed with these more optimistic predictions backed by publicity-conscious astronomers who should have heeded caution, prepared the public for this potentially unique event. Also condoning this wild optimism were publicists who, working with NASA, saw it as an opportunity to justify the large public expense then being incurred (and strongly criticised) in the Skylab programme at that time running at $4 million a week. In spite of their motives, the approaching comet was indeed a very suitable target for study outside the Earth's atmosphere by Skylab.

As the date for the comet's perihelion drew closer. the bandwagon of optimism in the popular press became unstoppable. By now the event was promoted to the status of a Barnum and Baily production: . . . Fancy-goods and T-shirt manufacturers saw the occasion as a heaven-sent opportunity for a commercial rip-off. One British company went so far as to register themselves as Comet Kohoutek Ltd in attempts to corner the market. The cranks, as always, were having a field-day and began to publish doom-watch pamphlets, much in the fashion their forebears had done with the advent of the Plague and the Fire comets of 1664 and 1665, and confidently predicted the end of the world. For the first time in publishing history, comet books, well-informed or otherwise, were selling in New York as fast as the latest fiction Pulitzer Prize winner. Airlines, keen to get into the act, promoted charter flights for the comet buffs who didn't want to miss out because of last-minute bad weather or cloud-outs. Kohoutek, himself a very modest man and innocent party to all the razzmatazz, was persuaded aboard the luxury cruise-liner *QE2*, sailing out from New York specially for this occasion, to lecture a rich, eager clientele who had taken passage on the recommendation that a view of the comet from the darkened skies of the North Atlantic would be truly memorable . . .

On schedule at the end of December 1973 the Skylab crew observed the comet from space just after its perihelion passage. By now it had become a brightish object, but at this time it was very badly placed for public view at ground level. Already, however, the earlier, and more wildly optimistic expectations were falling far short. The media soon suspected something was wrong . . . By the time the general public first viewed the comet, as it slowly emerged into the evening sky, it had dimmed to the general appearance of a fuzzy fourth magnitude star, not even properly visible to the naked eye. Out in the Atlantic, the special comet-watch cruise of the *QE2* was persistently dogged by bad weather and cloud, and for much of the time her passengers, including the discoverer himself, were below decks groaning with sea-sickness.

From the point of view of the man in the street, comet Kohoutek proved a very damp squib. As a result the public were now distrusting of astronomer's predictions. When comet West graced the morning skies in early March 1976, few could be tempted to desert their warm beds . . . As a result the doubting Thomases all missed out on a magnificent spectacle that even outrivalled comet Bennett.

Notwithstanding its poor public showing, Kohoutek's comet proved of great scientific interest. The comet was subject to an international 'Kohoutek Watch' by scientists equipped with a whole range of sophisticated space-age instrumentation never before applied to comet observations. It was scanned from the ground and in the air in the ultra-violet, infra-red, radio and visual wavebands. The infra-red observations showed the tail had a dust content less than Bennett's comet – perhaps only one-sixteenth as much – and again indicated that each comet is a unique object.

The presence of at least two organic molecules, methyle cyanide (CH_3CN) and hydrogen cyanide (HCN) were inferred from radio-astronomical observations, plus several other organic molecules which had not been specifically identified. Fred Hoyle and his colleague Chandra Wickramasinghe were to make much of these observations when later they announced their startling theories about the role of comets in the distribution of life in space. (*Chapter 10*).

*   *   *

By the mid-1970s Halley's comet, now at a distance of the orbit of Uranus, was accelerating inwards towards the Sun for its next perihelion timed for early February 1986. Already preparations were well under way to mount the most intensive observing programme ever afforded a comet.

The spate of brilliant, some even great, comets of the past decade had provided fresh, often tantalizing, clues about the chemistry and possible origins of what were physically still the most puzzling members of the solar family.

By this time it was widely accepted that the physical structure inside a comet's head could be likened to a discrete, solid mixture composed of ices and dust in the form of a loosely knit conglomerate. This provided the basis for the nucleus – the often star-like object seen at or near the centre of the head – which in bright comets emits jets, or envelopes, of nebulous material.

The basic icy-conglomerate idea had first been mooted back in the nineteenth century by a German astronomer named Hirn and the Englishman, Ranyard, but a more modern and advanced concept of it, circa 1950, was the independent brain-child of Fred Whipple, the doyen of American cometary astronomers.

Whipple visualized a comet as a kind of rotating 'dirty snowball' made up of a discrete 'hard' nucleus at its centre and packaged with such basic ingredients as water (H_2O), ammonia (NH_3), methane (CH_4), possibly carbon dioxide (CO_2) and dicyanogen (C_2H_2), plus other exotics and 'solid' dust particles. In texture the nucleus might be likened to a yeasty raisin bread.

Not everyone agreed with this idea. An alternative nineteenth-century model envisaged the structure of a comet to be a cloud of separate, loose particles but travelling together in orbit and compacted at the centre, providing the illusionary impression of a solid pseudo-nucleus. Perhaps not surprisingly, this particular comet model is appositely called the 'flying sandbank'. Its modern champion is the Cambridge astronomer Raymond Lyttleton. The flying-sandbank idea was much in vogue during the nineteenth century after it was discovered that comets were closely associated with spectacular meteor showers. For example, the Bielids connected with Biela's lost comet; the Leonids with the Tempel-Tuttle comet of 1866; and later the Eta Aquarids were found to be connected with Halley's comet. By the 1970s few astronomers favoured the flying-sandbank concept, for meteor streams as cometary debris are just as easily accommodated within the dirty-snowball idea.

With advances in the design and size of optical telescopes since the nineteenth century, there was always the chance that the question of which comet-model was the correct one might one day be settled by direct observation. In 1927, when the Pons-Winnecke comet came within 5.6 million km of the Earth, the French astronomer F. Baldet observed it carefully with the 60-cm Meudon refractor of the Paris Observatory and concluded that the comet's nucleus, if it existed at all, could not be larger than a few hundred metres in diameter. The more modern work of Elizabeth Roemer, using the 102-cm astrometric reflector of the Washington Naval Observatory, a telescope of exceptional definition, had set an *upper limit* and indicated that comet nuclei as monolithic bodies could not be *larger* than about 3 to 4 km for short-period comets and 7 to 8 km for long-period comets. Comet nuclei, however, on average are likely much smaller bodies.

Spectroscopy was still unable to settle the question of the fundamental chemical make-up of comets by earth-bound observation. While great advances had been made in studying the physical constituents of distant stars and galaxies, comets remained enigmatic. The spectroscope as applied to comets proved by no means as infallible as the camera, for by now it was realized that some emissions seen in comet spectra are simulated phenomena and in reality do not exist at all. Constituent parent molecules remained hard to identify, as they emit radiation in the infra-red and ultra-violet regions not available for study except outside the Earth's atmosphere. To complicate matters even further, molecules exist in unfamiliar terrestrial forms owing to the very low gas densities encountered in comets.

Clearly then, comets, by now, were recognized as ripe subjects for study by satellites or by space probes. The success of the probes to the Moon and Mars gave hope that by the mid-1980s, when Halley's comet was due, it might even be possible to make a close rendezvous with its mysterious icy nucleus . . .

Yet another important question unanswered was the origin of comets. During the nineteenth century the idea most favoured was that comets were objects captured by the Sun from regions outside the solar system.

Another idea was that comets were material ejected from the interiors of Jupiter and Saturn, or from the Sun itself.

Modern opinion had now swung to a more simple idea. Comets, it suggested, are the partially condensed primitive material left over after the planets were formed. Therefore they represent the 'fossilized', lighter factions of the original solar nebula – chemically much like the material that went into forming the outer planets Uranus and Neptune.

The Dutch astronomer J.H. Oort and his later disciples had worked out a theory that most of this remnant 'fossil' material – 'Oort's Cloud' – now lies as a vast ring of comets at the far boundaries of the solar system. According to Oort's theory we see new comets when dynamical interactions, caused by nearby stars or by massive planets like Uranus and Neptune, perturb distant comets and move them inwards to rendezvous with the Sun. Thus comets in the inner solar system are continually being replenished from this vast reservoir of distant material.

Comets, then, as suggested above, may in reality be remnant pristine material of the solar system and represent a class of original bodies similar in composition to the outer giant planets.

Notes

[1] In the 49 instances coloured comets are mentioned in Chinese records, 23 are recorded as white, 20 bluish, 4 red or reddish-yellow and 2 greenish. According to Seneca the comet of 146 BC was 'as large as the Sun' and 'its disc a fiery red'. Pliny writes of early comets 'whose mace was the colour of blood'. According to Arago, the comets of 662 and 1526 were 'of a beautiful red'.

During the Middle Ages and the Renaissance, some very colourful comets were reported, and gold is a colour frequently alluded to. This was undoubtedly due to the presence of sodium. Comets rich in nickel would certainly appear greenish. Such a marked greenish tint was actually noted in the tail of the bright southern comet discovered in 1967 (VII). Perhaps the most remarkable are the 'blue' comets of 1217 which Pingré cites. Another, in 1476, was 'pale blue bordering upon black'; a still later comet was described as 'terrible and of a blackish hue'.

Various meteorological effects may easily influence the apparent colour of a comet. Brilliant comets are often observed near the Sun and are frequently low in the sky at the time of observation. A brilliant sunset would certainly induce a reddish or even a greenish-bluish tint, and fine dust ejected into the atmosphere by volcanoes may at times exaggerate the colour effect. Certainly at the time of a total lunar eclipse 'blue' Moons are not that uncommon. Although one day a genuine blue or red comet may come along to astound us, on present evidence it seems unlikely. In the past it is probable that an unusual colour was often invoked by a chronicler to add dramatic emphasis to his description and was applied in a metaphorical rather than a strictly literal sense.

[2] The second bright comet of 1957 – comet Mrkos 1957 V(d) – is entered in the record books under the single name of the Czech Anton Mrkos, one of the most successful of the modern comet hunters. However, the comet was independently discovered as a naked-eye object by several others. One of its early co-discoverers was a British schoolboy whose father's telegram announcing his son's discovery lay unopened for a week on a desk at the Royal Greenwich Observatory owing to the British Bank Holiday! In those days the holiday fell in the first week of August. Apparently the telegram was addressed to the Astronomer Royal, who was absent, and staff thought it to be a private communication. When it was opened, it was already too late. Mrkos's name is now attached to this comet as his announcement was the first to reach the International Astronomical Union Telegraph Bureau then housed in Copenhagen. This was a sad episode, denying an alert, keen-eyed youngster the opportunity to immortalize his own name with a comet. One wonders how Messier would have reacted to losing a comet in similar circumstances.

[3] Another famous Sungrazer which was seen to divide was the comet 1882 II. Before the eyes of astronomers, its nucleus split into four distinct parts – appearing to one observer like 'glistening pearls on a string'. When it graced the morning sky in October that year, it was watched by E.E. Barnard then engaged in amateur comet hunting. Previously he had discovered two comets, 1881 VI and 1882 III, and was busy trying to keep the wolf from the door with prize money for comet discoveries then currently on offer by the wealthy American H.H. Warner. Barnard's mind was constantly preoccupied by comets, and it was now he had a remarkable experience: 'My thoughts,' he recalled, 'must have run strongly on comets during that time, for one night when thoroughly worn out I set my alarm clock and lay down for a short sleep. Possibly it was the noise of the clock that set my wits to work . . . or the worry of the mortgage and the hope of finding another comet or two to wipe it out. Whatever the cause I had the most wonderful dream. I thought I was looking at the sky which was filled with comets, long tailed and short tailed and with no tails at all . . . I had just begun to gather the crop when the alarm went off and the blessed vision of comets vanished. I took my telescope out in the yard and began sweeping the heavens to the southwest of the great comet in search for (new) comets. Presently I ran upon a very cometary looking object where there was no known nebula. Looking more carefully I saw several others in the field of view. Moving the telescope about I found that there must have been 10 to 15 comets at this point within the space of a few degrees. Before dawn killed them I located six or eight of them. That morning I sent a telegram to Dr Lewis Swift, notifying him of the

discovery of six or eight "comets" at a certain position. Whether he thought I was trying to form a comet trust or had suddenly gone demented has never been clear to me, for he unfortunately did not forward the telegram. The observations were amply verified, however, both in this country and in Europe, by other observers who saw some of these bodies. Unquestionably they were a group of small comets or fragments that had been disrupted from the great comet, perhaps when it whirled round the Sun and grazed its surface several weeks earlier with the speed of nearly four hundred miles a second. The association of this dream with the reality has always seemed a strange thing to me.'

Barnard's observations were no figment of the imagination and were indeed confirmed by Julius Schmidt at the Athens Observatory, and by others elsewhere.

10 · Comets and Life

. . . if comets in the distant past shed life onto the Earth, we have to consider the possibility that comets were still doing so today . . . was life in the form of primitive bacteria still reaching the Earth? And could viruses even be derived from comets?

HEN COSMOLOGIST Fred Hoyle and his equally eminent co-author Chandra Wickramasinghe published these suggestions in the late 1970s and added that Halley's comet itself was likely involved in the periodic spread of pandemics on Earth, the ideas of the medieval astrologers were elevated to scientific verisimilitude.

Even Hoyle and Wickramasinghe realized that their most open-minded readership would have initial doubts about swallowing such time-worn heresies. 'The ideas seemed preposterous,' the authors wrote, 'but in science one must steel oneself not to decide the correctness or otherwise of ideas according to subjective prejudice. In science, fact reigns supreme . . .'

So what were the facts?

The genesis of Hoyle's and Wickramasinghe's interests about life in space date back to the early 1960s. Astronomers then were trying to understand the nature of the grains of matter spread out in interstellar space which caused fogging of more distant starlight on photographic plates.

One early theory about these grains had been that they were tiny ice-crystals, but spectral analysis ruled this out. They had to be something more exotic than just ice – something containing the elements hydrogen, oxygen, nitrogen and carbon believed to be present in deep cosmic space.

143

As the years ticked by, however, researchers were unable to identify correctly the matter producing the observed spectrum.

Hoyle and Wickramasinghe, following their own line of research, now decided the grains originated from solid carbon in the form of graphite, yet in the end this idea looked unlikely and was discarded. Later they started to think about the possibility of organic, carbon-based materials, but again with little initial success. Then, by chance, they came across the infra-red spectrum of mundane, everyday cotton which, as a candidate for comparison with the interstellar spectra, looked better than anything they had checked before. But, cotton in space? No, not exactly, but cotton is mainly carbohydrate, reasoned the authors, and the direct inference was that out in space the elusive grains were structures as complicated as terrestrial carbohydrates.

They spent some time pondering the problem and trying to work out how carbohydrates could be produced in space by non-biological processes.

In the meantime radio telescopes had detected emissions from space of organic molecules such as formaldehyde, acetaldehyde, formic acid and others like methanimine and methylamine. These were detected at wavelengths inaccessible to optical telescopes in sources like the Trifid Nebula located near the centre of the Milky Way.

The watershed in Hoyle's and Wickramasinghe's thinking was 1977. If the mystery was to be solved, a radical approach was needed. It was now they crossed the boundary from orthodox astronomy into the realms of the heretical non-orthodox. It was time to come to grips with the problem and recognize that the grains out in deep cosmic space not only contained complex organic molecules like those detected by the radio telescopes *but were living bacteria-like organisms.*

Their grain size was just about right to match the spectral characteristics of complete bacterial cells on Earth, and they provided a better fit than the earlier cotton spectrum.

Eureka! QED. Not quite.

While Hoyle and Wickramasinghe believed they were on the threshold of a new concept about life in space, consensus believed otherwise. The spectra themselves were inconclusive evidence on which to base such a theory. The history of science is full of wonderful new theories erected on the slenderest of evidence only to be demolished in due course as nature in her perversity has a cunning way of booby-trapping man's road to knowledge.

As far as the established scientific community were concerned, their claims about the grains were of interest but highly speculative at best; hardly anyone was prepared to accept the concept just because so far no one else had come up with a better idea to explain the nature of the grains.

Undeterred by criticism, Hoyle and Wickramasinghe entered the scientific wilderness and began to elaborate, through a series of books, their highly personal life-in-space ideas. Initially their goal was to show that, contrary to established thinking which had life evolving on Earth from a primitive self-generating 'biological soup', it arrived *ready*-made from space.

But there were problems about its mode of transportation. If living bacteria were out in space, the task was to find a mechanism to get them carried into the solar system to seed the inner planets.

They had several choices. They could opt for the idea that life germs were part of the original solar nebula which condensed to form the planets and other bodies in the solar system and so were there/here from the start of things. To some degree this indeed was part of their premise, for it followed that organic interstellar grains would constitute part of any initial nebula. Alternatively, they could also choose to cite the mechanism of meteorite-falls. By now meteorite research was providing tantalizing clues, demonstrating that the precursors to life, at least, existed outside the Earth's environment.

One can understand the reluctance of Hoyle and Wickramasinghe to choose meteorites, for while the right kinds of meteorites (carbonaceous chondrites) might have been very abundant in the past, the evidence for life via meteorites was conjectural and provided too many constraints to all-embracing ideas. This was a trap to avoid. The notion that life was present in the initial solar nebula was the right approach; this source itself was enough to support their theory. However, their prime target for the future was nothing less than a frontal attack on the tenets of Darwinian evolution. Not only did they see life on Earth as the product of seeding from space from the very beginning, they also saw it continuing to reach Earth through time – battering at the door of our planet into the immediate present and providing the mechanisms that determined the evolution and the subsequent diversification of incumbent species.

*   *   *

Ignoring earlier non-scientific speculations of people like the lexicographer Noah Webster, modern ideas about life from space date back to nineteenth-century scientists like William Thomson (later Lord Kelvin).

When Thomson delivered his inaugural address to the British Association in 1871 and put forward the idea that life on Earth could have its origin from seeds borne here by meteorites and then coupled this statement with another, reminding his audience that meteors were remnants of comets and their tails, there were those listening who believed they were victims of a presidential joke.

Richard Proctor, a popular astronomical correspondent of the period and then Secretary to the Royal Astronomical Society, was one of those present who believed it was an ill-timed leg-pull, made in bad taste, and perpetrated by the Scot with the foreknowledge and indulgence of all the other noted Scots in the audience in order to hoax the Sassenachs present.

Later realizing it was probably *not* meant as a joke, Proctor was still unsure how seriously he should treat the statement. Writing for his own lay audience in the *St Paul's Magazine* for September 1871, he remarks: '. . . if this new theory should be accepted, we have reason to regard with apprehension the too close approach of one of these visitants; because, if one comet supplied the seeds of the living things now existing on the world, another may supply myriads of seeds of undesirable living things; and perhaps subsequent struggle for life may not result in the survival of the fittest.'

Proctor, a sometime cosmologist himself, was anticipating Hoyle's and Wickramasinghe's thesis of the following century, but it is doubtful if the later authors ever set eyes on this earlier review article. Their antecedents stem partly from Kelvin, but mostly from the Swedish chemist Svante Arrhenius who, in 1907, in his book *Worlds in the Making*, proposed the panspermia hypothesis in which he suggested that simple forms of life had drifted from world to world, propelled through the medium of interstellar space by radiation pressure which had recently been identified as a very significant force at work in producing cometary tails when comets come near the Sun.

There can be no doubt that Hoyle, in particular, saw Arrhenius as an image of himself: a scientist of rare intelligence and original thinking, always his own man and at odds with his scientific peers. Arrhenius, with his heretical ideas on electrolytes, had cocked a snook at the Swedish establishment. Then later in 1903 these previously unacceptable ideas earned him the Nobel Prize for chemistry!

In developing his theory, Arrhenius took cognizance of Kelvin's ideas and also those of a German scientist, H.E. Richter, who, among others, reversed the idea of Kelvin – arguing that life from Earth might itself be transferred elsewhere to other planets by meteorites brushing and then bouncing off our atmosphere during which time they picked up living cells. Arrhenius was severely handicapped in developing a truly comprehensive theory because of the poor state of physics in the early years of the twentieth century. He wondered, for example, how living cells wandering in space, propelled only by radiation pressure, could survive long enough on the long journeys from one star to another.

His speculations were unacceptable to the scientific community at large. He might be a Nobel Prize winner, but he was a chemist and not a biologist or astronomer. Why didn't he stick to chemistry and leave the problem of life's origins to those whose training gave them a better understanding of it? This negative argument was to echo again in criticisms raised against Hoyle and Wickramasinghe. Nevertheless, Arrhenius's ideas were vulnerable to criticism. Ultraviolet light, it was pointed out, was positively lethal to his extraterrestrial spores travelling in space; later, when the deadly cosmic rays – unknown in Arrhenius's time – were identified, his theory was damned again and consigned to the limbo of the scientific scrap-heap. It stayed there until, in much modified form, it was resurrected by Hoyle and Wickramasinghe in the late 1970s.

*   *   *

The advent of comet Kohoutek in 1973-4 impressed Hoyle if not the public at large. The comet was examined at wave-lengths in the ultra-violet, visual, infra-red and radio wave-bands. Emission-bands corresponding to many atomic species and simple molecules seen in previous comets were confirmed, including carbon (C_2), cyanogen (CN), methylidyne (CH), the hydroxyl radical (OH) and the amino group (NH_2). In Kohoutek at least two organic molecules, methyl cyanide (CH_3 CN) and hydrogen cyanide (HCN) were also inferred from radioastronomical observations. In addition there were several other radio-frequency lines present, presumably arising from organic molecules still awaiting identification. All in all, it was an impressive list of material and in the form of a comet just what he and Wickramasinghe were looking for as a highly mobile source for life. Comets had the added advantage that they moved in highly eccentric orbits which caused them at aphelion to pass beyond the normal outer regions of the solar system; on the other hand, at perihelion, they were close to the Sun and the inner planets and subject to strong radiation pressure as well as solar bombardment in the guise of corpuscular particles forming the solar wind. Might not then the dusty tails of comets be the actual spreaders of cosmic

147

spores and bacteria that are carried into the Earth's atmosphere as micro-meteorites when the Earth passes through a comet's tail or intersects its path?

Hoyle and Wickramasinghe had never previously been much interested in comets. Like other cosmologists they had considered them as playing but a minor role in the shaping of the cosmos. Now, however, things were different, comets *per se* could be requisitioned as the ideal vehicles for transporting those all-important interstellar grains to the inner regions of the solar system on a periodic basis. Their arguments took the line that when the solar system was created 4.6 eons ago, hundreds of millions of comets were formed as ice-balls and remained circling in the outer regions. Subsequently, on the surface of these ice-balls (comets) were deposited interstellar grains which grew as mantles – perhaps up to one kilometre thick. Collisions between comets as they were jostled about would release energy; any melt-water trapped near the ice-core boundary would then provide liquid nurseries for cosmic spores and bacteria that could remain preserved for millions of years.

In a later development of their idea, Hoyle and Wickramasinghe see comets more as *carriers* rather than as original reservoirs of genetic material. Either way, these onboard packages remain preserved long enough to survive the day when their host in outer space is perturbed by a passing star and starts to head inwards for a rendezvous with the Sun and Earth. Thus comets transformed into short periods, like Halley's comet, would periodically dissipate their organic cargoes under the erosive influence of sunlight. To explain germ-spread and subsequent diseases on Earth, Hoyle and Wickramasinghe cite, in the case of Halley's comet, that outbreaks may be expected at intervals varying from seventy-four to seventy-nine years to match variations in its orbital period.[1]

The fact that Hoyle is a superb mathematician who is able to manipulate numbers at the drop of a hat to support his and Wickramasinghe's unorthodox ideas makes them a difficult target for critical attack by non-numerate biologists who oppose them. For the same reason it made Hoyle a formidable opponent of the archaeologists during the Stonehenge controversy of the 1960s when he stepped in to offer mathematical confirmation that the four-thousand-year-old monument could work extremely well as an astronomical observatory. His often statistical approach to evolution, citing, for example, that Darwin's theory is mathematically impossible, makes it difficult for opponents to answer in relevant, numerate counter-argument. Yet Hoyle and Wickramasinge are sometimes very careless and naive in their descriptive exposition and often misquote established facts – which leaves them vulnerable to accusations that their claims are unscientific.

At other times Hoyle has a succinct way of marshalling a battery of cool, logical argument; neither is he afraid of dropping in provocative, casual asides like the very original theory that the human nose has evolved its characteristic shape to help it avoid drawing in harmful bacteria falling from the sky. Has a biologist/zoologist a better idea?[2]

Hoyle and Wickramasinghe believe that biologists who opt for life's origins *on Earth* take a narrow, pre-Copernican, blinkered view of the matter. They point out that the almost unlimited synthesizing laboratories of space offer infinitely more opportunities than those afforded on a primitive Earth. Biologists have to admit reluctantly that while the experiments of S.L. Miller and H.C. Urey in the 1950s showed how a primitive Earth-generated broth *might* begin a chain resulting in higher life-forms, it did not prove that conditions on Earth were uniquely favourable.

With the modern evidence provided by meteorites and radio telescopes that life's precursors at least exist outside our biosphere, many space-age scientists would agree in principle with Hoyle and Wickramasinghe and look to realms beyond our own planet for life's true origins; however, displacing orthodox Darwinian theory as a mechanism for species change with an on-going flux of cosmic spores shed by comets remains heretical and a much more contentious matter. This fundamental evolutionary question, nevertheless, is open to speculation until proved otherwise. It is the more fanciful ideas of comets like Halley's in the role of an interplanetary 'flu machine, and Hoyle's and Wickramasinghe's startling explanations about the historical pattern of epidemic infection, that leave most scientists gasping. Yet an eminent open-minded medical authority much respected in the field, when asked to express a clear verdict about the probabilities of cosmic-inspired pandemics, hesitated before admitting: 'It is very difficult to argue against, isn't it . . .' but then added wryly, 'as a medical microbiologist it is my duty to give a clear verdict on the theory . . . My verdict, then, is: it can't be true – *or can it?*'[3]

Notes

[1] Hoyle's and Wickramasinghe's ideas are set out in several books, beginning with their seminal work *Lifecloud* (1978) in which they presented their basic premise about the nature of organic molecules in space, along with the idea of life first arriving on Earth from interstellar regions. In their next book, more

evocatively titled *Diseases from Space* (1979), they now presented arguments and 'facts' to underpin a new thesis that viruses and bacteria responsible for infectious diseases of plants and animals arrive on Earth from space via comets. In addition their further claim was that apart from harmful effects, some viruses and bacteria were responsible in the past not only for the origin of life on Earth but also acted as agencies for its subsequent evolution. In their later books *Evolution from Space* (1981) and *Space Travellers – the Bringers of Life* (1981) their evolution thesis was now more fully developed as a direct attack on Darwinian theory and it revealed the authors as flying the flag of the old-fashioned creationists. In 1983 the arguments were taken one step further with publication, under Hoyle's independent authorship, of *The Intelligent Universe*, subtitled: *A New View of Creation and Evolution* in which his idea of a super-intelligence at work in the universe is set out.

[2] Nevertheless, in respect to this off-the-cuff insight about the evolution of the human nose, one cannot help being reminded of a passage in Voltaire's famous satire *Candide* when the erudite Professor Pangloss remarks equally glibly: 'It is demonstrable that all is necessarily for the best end. Observe that the nose has been formed to bear spectacles . . .'

[3] Many distinguished scientists have refrained from offering any kind of criticism and prefer the wall-of-silence approach to register their disdain of Hoyle's and Wickramasinghe's entire thesis. In their view their heresies are no more scientific than those contained in Velikovsky's first book *Worlds in Collision* which created a furore in the early 1950s. They believe that offering criticism is time-wasting and nugatory. They emphasize the two authors repeatedly misrepresent Darwin's ideas and they are totally ill equipped by their training to dabble in realms beyond their own disciplines.

Hoyle, in particular, remains immune to attacks on his scholarship. He has a genuine polymathic mind and has proven he can encompass the interdisciplinary approach to problem-solving. In the fashion of his celebrated predecessors like anthropologist Sir James Frazer and the astronomer Sir Norman Lockyer, he had no compunction of invading others' scholastic domains, ignoring the rigid scientific demarcations to root out new facts; if the specialists do not like it, it's just too bad! One suspects that Hoyle, like his contentious predecessors, subscribes to the sometimes mischievous view that one should not let one's ignorance of a particular discipline stop one from taking it by the throat to see what it has to say for itself.

11 · Rendezvous with Halley's Comet

Y THE MID-1970s the next perihelion passage of Halley's comet was only a decade away. Already computers were busy working out the complex equations of its motion, trying to predict the exact time. Technology had made enormous advances since 1909; tasks which had taken Cowell and Crommelin, and their three helpers, weeks of labour to calculate could be printed out at the press of a few keys in fractions of a minute. While the tedium was now removed from the exercise, the new electronic machines were still only artefacts; they could only perform within the limits of the accuracy of the observational data fed into them. With Halley's comet there were still problems about the magnitude of the non-gravitational forces at work that had puzzled Cowell and Crommelin and had led to a disparity of three days between prediction and actual perihelion date.

The non-gravitational forces in comets – not predictable by Kepler's laws – were by now better understood. They were believed to be caused by an outgassing in the comet's icy nucleus producing a rocket-effect leading to accelerations or decelerations in orbital motion. Indeed, the presence and action of non-gravitational forces was taken to confirm that Whipple's idea of a discrete icy nucleus was the more correct comet-model, for it is difficult to see how such a rocket-effect could arise in a loose agglomeration of particles as proposed by the alternative sandbank idea.

During the 1960s the first plans were drawn up by various agencies for future fly-by missions to suitable periodic comets. In the late '60s and early '70s, space vehicles in orbit looking at comets discovered the vast envelopes of hydrogen gas surrounding them – totally invisible from Earth-bound observatories. It was clear by this time that a close fly-by mission, or an actual rendezvous with the inner nuclear regions, was the only hope of ever determining the true physical make-up of cometary bodies and their possible close relatives, the Earth-crossing Apollo asteroids thought by some to be defunct comets.

The prime target for the future was Halley's comet in 1985-6. It was a prime target for two reasons: it was the most famous of all comets, and it was probably a large comet in comparison with most periodic ones. Other comets shortlisted were P/Encke which was favourably placed in 1974 and again in 1980; P/d'Arrest in 1976; P/Kopff in 1983; and P/Arend-Rigaux in 1984.

Clearly a practice-run at a comet before 1985-6 would help iron out any wrinkles for a later probe to Halley's comet. In the interim years, however, constraints by NASA on space-mission budgets decided them to concentrate their efforts on planetary explorations using the Mariner, Pioneer and Voyager probes. The Soviet Union likewise, although long interested in comet probes, also limited its activities to the planets.

It was clear to comet-mission planners that compared with planetary missions those to comets faced several added difficulties. A major problem is pinpointing a comet's path with sufficient precision to make an intercept. In most cases the non-gravitational forces affecting comets are small yet significant enough; and if a comet goes anywhere near Jupiter before its next rendezvous with the Sun, the perturbing effects of the giant planet may make the calculations of its intercept, without later corrections to its predicted ephemeris, a hit-and-miss exercise.

Among the comets picked out, P/Arend-Rigaux, due in 1984, was the best candidate for it was the one having the least problems determining its run-in orbit. As veteran comet computer Brian Marsden pointed out to mission planners, it had not made a close approach to Jupiter for 900 years, and as there appeared to be no non-gravitational forces at work disturbing it, its path was usually very predictable. But that was 1984 and a date too near to the ultimate mission just eighteen months later to profit from experience.

The most errant of the short-listed comets was P/d'Arrest; here Marsden pointed out that if a space vehicle were launched to intercept it on the basis of a prediction ephemeris before the comet was resighted photographically (when its ephemeris could be corrected), the ranging could be uncertain by as much as 50,000 km, perhaps even more. Comet P/Encke, however, in spite of the non-gravitational forces at work on it, might be predicted with more accuracy since with large modern telescopes it had been followed along its orbit to near its aphelion point at a distance of 4 AU where it was seen as a dim $20\overset{m}{.}5$ object.

If Halley's comet could be tracked in from a similar great distance, this would make any launch more accurate. But Halley's comet presents two main problems. Unlike the other comets under consideration, it has a retrograde, or indirect, orbit (opposite to that of the planets) which poses difficulties for a fly-by. For example, it involves an encounter velocity with a space probe of some 60-70 km per second as against 0.1 km per second for P/Kopff and 12 km per second for P/d'Arrest – both of which have direct, planet-like orbits. In addition to this, Halley's comet has the enigmatical factor of significant non-gravitational forces affecting it.

The most sophisticated of the alternative forward-planned missions to Halley's comet was one not waiting for the comet to be resighted photographically before launch. This was the so-called rendezvous mission whereby the space probe would be dispatched from Earth in late 1977 and made to encounter Jupiter a year later. From this encounter the probe's orbit would be changed from direct to retrograde motion and set on a path to bring it alongside the comet early in 1985. Using this method, the probe and the comet would cruise side by side during the run-in and permit observations of the inner parts of the head at very close range.

In its previous apparition, earlier in the century, Halley's comet had been spotted 249 days before perihelion in mid-April 1910, then after perihelion it was followed at Helwan, in Egypt, for 396 days, making a total of 645 observation days, surprisingly 5 days less than during the 1835-6 apparition.

If the more conventional direct-orbit probes were to be used and it could be resighted about 400 days before perihelion, this, it was judged, would provide a series of pre-launch check positions so that corrections could be incorporated into the ephemeris of the comet to make targeting more accurate. Thus provisionally a very conservative expectation date for recovery was set for January 1985 . . .

However, by the second half of the 1970s, observers were a lot more ambitious in their resighting predictions. Since the turn of the century, telescopes equipped with electronic accessories, as well as computers, had made enormous technological advances. Even so, it was a great surprise to most when observers with access to two of the largest telescopes in the

United States began their searches as early as November 1977, more than eight years before the comet was expected! At this time Halley's comet was estimated to be dimmer than 26^m. What was clear, however, was that the spirit of Farmer Palitzsch lived on . . .

*   *   *

For the 1985-6 apparition several computers made independent researches into the past apparitions of Halley's comet to try to refine the predicted date for perihelion due to occur early in February 1986.

One of these studies originated from the NASA Jet Propulsion Laboratory at Pasadena and was published by Donald K. Yeomans as 'An Observer's Guide'. This included an ephemeris 1981-87 to assist those astronomers participating in the world-wide International Halley Watch programme organized under the auspices of the International Astronomical Union. In his study Yeomans utilized a total of 885 past observations beginning with that of Kepler's on 28 September 1607 and ending with a photographic one dated 24 May 1911. Yeomans also incorporated allowances for the non-gravitational forces at work on the comet, spanning the four centuries of motion since Kepler's time.

A more in-depth study was that made sometime earlier by T. Kiang, who retraced the path of the comet through earlier Chinese observations back to 240 BC. Kiang's interest in the comet began in 1969 after becoming intrigued by Ho Peng Yoke's catalogue, which provided a set of unique observations on ten specific dates for the return of AD 837 not available to Cowell and Crommelin earlier in the century. Using a modern computer, Kiang repeated Cowell's and Crommelin's pre-electronic-age calculations, adopting much the same methods but incorporating a number of refinements that included perturbations in all three dimensions for all the major planets.

Kiang had the advantage he was able to read and resolve early oriental texts. By adopting a mixture of computative and graphical analysis, he traced the orbit back through each apparition. Much of his time was spent on a detailed re-examination of the original records rather than on second-hand Western translations which others had usually relied on. He was able to clear up several previous ambiguities respecting early Chinese observations and concluded that by the ninth century AD Chinese astronomers had been able to measure a comet's position with an accuracy to one half of a degree, a feat not accomplished in Europe until well after the Renaissance.

Kiang confirmed that the return of AD 837 was a very noteworthy one. On 9 April that year the comet approached the Earth to within 0.04 AU and moved 60° across the sky in 24 hours. Chinese observers reported its tail to be over '80 feet' long or, as Kiang translated, equivalent to more than 100° in length, rivalling the length reported in 1910 but not then seen to best advantage. His researches also shed light on the length of the tail during its famous apparition in 1066. Chinese observations had spoken of the comet passing through various stars, and Kiang interpreted this as their method of describing tail length rather than the movement of the comet itself. Applying this idea to what the observers actually saw on 24 April 1066, it indicated the tail then stretched from horizon to horizon and hung directly northwards, passing through the north celestial pole. The next day it was still a magnificent sight as the tail spread itself across the constellations of Auriga, through Gemini, Leo, Virgo, Libra and Scorpius.

Joseph L. Brady is another computer whose work on recalculating the orbit of the comet is of great interest. Brady's work extends the apparitions from 1986 back as far as 2646 BC. It was Brady who had earlier claimed that the anomalous motions of Halley's comet were due, in part, to the presence of a yet unseen massive planet lying beyond Pluto. Although he computed a rough ephemeris for the supposed path of this body, to date all searches for it have proved negative.

In respect to his work on the comet itself, Brady again drew attention to the problem that all previous efforts to link past apparitions relying only on Newtonian equations had failed each time. This had resulted in at least a three- or four-day error in predicting perihelion and always with the same directional bias. By including in his calculations what he referred to as a secular term (i.e. an allowance for non-gravitational forces) to the usual equations of motion, he and colleagues, making use of about 5,000 observations, claimed to have successfully linked back the four apparitions of 1910, 1835, 1759 and 1682.

Continuing this integration programme further back in time, Brady also claimed to have been able to fix earlier apparitions with a numerical accuracy greater than that found in ancient observational records. The work was extended to retrace thirty-four apparitions previous to that of 87 BC, the earliest date for Halley's comet identified by Cowell and Crommelin with certainty. Thus he took the comet's supposed history as far back as 2646 BC.

In apparitions previous to 240 BC, which was Kiang's limit based on reliable Chinese observations, Brady admitted that any confirmation of a sighting of a comet with a computed apparition in the appropriate year is beset by the problem of recognizing in inscriptions what he refers to as 'the cometary metaphor'. Even this admission understates the difficulties. Scholars have long appreciated one may read into early Babylonian texts any manner of phenomena to suit a particular theory; they frequently, and hotly, dispute each others' claims about what a particular inscription may actually refer to. What is often forgotten is that in the later Babylonian astronomical diaries, where accounts are much clearer, *there is not a single reference to a comet to be found anywhere!* In the older, more ambiguous, texts, some of which in turn are only Babylonian copies of earlier texts and contain gross errors and lacunas, it is difficult at times even to disentangle planetary names and the names of a few bright stars and constellations.

Yeomans and Kiang had also performed much the same backtracking exercise as Brady and speculatively traced out the comet's supposed apparitions over 3,000 years. Yeomans's approach was more cautious than Brady's, and he stopped his integration at what he claimed was a return in 1404 BC where Brady cited the year 1445 BC, a difference of over 41 years between them!

Brady's less conventional methodology involves the use of a variable constant (a contradiction in terms), and this certainly leads to differences between the authors in claimed perihelion dates back in prehistory. Brady, perhaps with some justification, explains differences in some perihelion times from those of Kiang's (based on actual Chinese observations) are due to the fact that the ancient Chinese calendrical systems cannot be as easily correlated with the Julian and Gregorian calendars as some might suppose.

According to Brady's calculations the comet back in dim prehistory sometimes returned to perihelion in a shorter period than the *observed* all-time record one of 74.42 years between 1835-1910. In 1646 BC, according to Brady's reckoning, the return took only 73.08 years and that between 917 BC and 844 BC 73.16 years; there were also several other cited instances of returns in less than 74 years.

*   *   *

By January 1981 the comet was moving unseen between the orbits of Uranus and Saturn, now gradually picking up speed and accelerating inwards. Round this time its predicted brightness was estimated to be fainter than 25^m. Its inward path lay among the rich star fields of the

Milky Way on the borders of Canis Minor and Monoceros. As seen from the Earth its daily shift among the background stars would be very slow. While theoretically the comet was now just within range of the largest modern telescopes equipped with image-intensifiers, the task of identifying it from among thousands of other faint, anonymous stellar images at the limit of visibility was like looking for a needle.

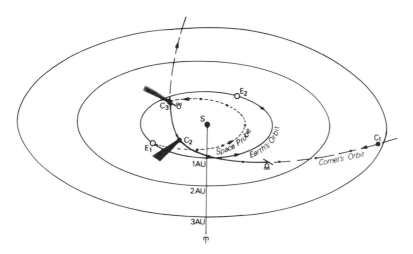

Fig. 13   A typical space probe to Halley's comet 1985-6. There are several alternative methods to enable a probe to make a rendezvous with the comet. In this example the probe is launched 210 days earlier from the Earth (E_1). C_1 is the position of Halley's comet at the time of probe launch. C_2 is the position of Halley's comet at the time of its perihelion passage (9 February 1986). E_2 and C_3 are the respective positions of the Earth and Halley's comet when the probe and the comet rendezvous (210 days after launch). (S = Sun; ♈ = First point in Aries used in orbital computations; ☊ and ☋ are the ascending and descending nodes respectively – or the points where the comet crosses the plane of the ecliptic.) The intervals between the black dots along the orbits of the comet and space probe represent 30-day periods after launch. Refer also to Appendix 3 for explanation of a comet's orbital geometry.

By this time the various comet-mission planners, who were still in the running for a probe to Halley's comet, were feverishly mounting their behind-the-scenes programmes. NASA, to the surprise of many, now declared it had no firm plans for a unique Halley mission. They were in fact reserving their options for a pre-empt fly-by mission to the favourably placed P/Giacobini-Zinner comet in 1985, using a previously launched probe, the International Comet Explorer, which, it was estimated, would have just enough fuel left to reposition itself into a fly-by orbit to Halley's comet in 1986 when it would pass at a distance of 30 million km.

Those who did have firm plans were the European Space Agency (ESA), the Japanese Institute of Space and Astronomical Science (ISAS) and the Soviet Union (*see Appendix 1*).

Although the search for the returning comet had begun in 1977, by 1981 there was still no sight of it. It would now be accelerating in towards Saturn's orbit, but so far the myriads of faint background stars in our own galaxy had rendered it anonymous. Even with an object as important as Halley's comet, scheduled telescope time for the interested parties was severely limited. By now, however, observers with access to the world's largest telescopes were engaged in an unofficial race to be first to resight it and so add their names to those of Farmer Palitzsch, Father Dumouchel and Dr Max Wolf.

Telescopes taking part in the hunt included the giant Soviet 6-metre telescope, the 5.08-metre Hale telescope at Mt Palomar, a 4.5-metre telescope in Arizona, three 4-metre telescopes in Arizona, others in Australia and South America, a 3-metre at the Lick Observatory and the 2.7-metre telescope at the MacDonald Observatory. Never before had such a battery of large telescopes been directed to the resighting of one comet.

In December 1981, in the transparent mountain air at Kitt Peak, Arizona, a concerted effort was mounted to find the returning comet, using the 4-metre telescope coupled to a very sensitive electronic image-intensifier. This arrangement was capable of picking up any faint object to a limit of 24^m3. Nevertheless, despite careful scrutiny, the telescope and its advanced equipment failed to reveal any slow-moving stranger lurking among the faint star fields.

The months rolled by, 1981 turned into 1982; then in the autumn of 1982, two keen astronomers at Mt Palomar, G. Edward Danielson and David C. Jewitt, were able to 'borrow' observing time from colleagues scheduled to use the famous 5.08-metre Hale telescope on other programmes.

Nowadays the night skies around Mt Palomar are plagued by sky fogging owing to street lighting in nearby towns. But, when conditions are good, the Hale telescope is a superb performer and coupled with an image-intensifier is capable of detecting objects to the ultimate limit of 25^m.

The first early-morning session available to them was on 16 October 1982 when the pair installed an electric charge-coupled device (an intensifier) at the prime focus of the 5.08-metre Hale telescope. At this time it was calculated the comet was at a distance of 1.6 thousand million kilometres from the Sun, and according to predictions it should be slightly brighter than in December 1981. Over an interval of one-and-a-half hours the two observers made five eight-minute exposures in yellow light; then, when twilight was rapidly coming on and time fast running out, they managed to obtain two further exposures in red light.

By the end of their early-morning session, Danielson and Jewitt were holding their breath. A quick check had revealed that on each exposure they had made there was a tiny slow-moving image which approximated to the ephemeris positions predicted by several computers. The images, however, were very faint and estimated to be about 24^m2, just above the threshold limit of the telescope.

After communicating their findings to Brian Marsden, incumbent Director at the IAU clearing-house for astronomical discoveries at Cambridge, Massachusetts, the problem now was deciding whether the images were those of the comet or alternatively those of a previously undiscovered faint asteroid. This latter alternative could perhaps explain the shift in motion of about 3 ½ seconds of arc over which the object had travelled during the course of their observations. But there was a sure clue about the motion of Halley's comet: it moves in a retrograde orbit, the opposite way round to the major planets and the asteroids. In that part of the sky observed by Jewitt and Danielson, any asteroid, Marsden decided, would appear to shift *eastwards*; the object found was shifting towards the *southwest*. In Marsden's opinion there was little doubt that the two Palomar observers had resighted the comet.

In 1758, Palitzsch had resighted Halley's comet less than three months prior to perihelion; in 1835, Father Dumouchel's observations were just over three months previous to it while in 1909, Max Wolf had photographed it seven-and-a-half months before. This time the two Palomar astronomers had smashed all records in finding it three years and four months before it was due to make its closest rendezvous with the Sun.

Nevertheless, confirmation was still required. Attempts were made three mornings later using the same telescope. As expected, no images were found in the places previously occupied by the moving object on 16 October, and this added confirmation to the reality of the earlier observations. Unfortunately, by now the comet was too close to one of the brighter field stars whose dazzling image overpowered any feeble light from the comet. In due course, however, confirmation was made, and now its position was known exactly, other telescopes of much smaller aperture were able to pick it up and then follow it.

Check calculations showed that the computers who had taken into

159

account the non-gravitational forces at work on the comet had this time almost got it right. The comet would arrive at perihelion 9.3 UT February 1986. Yeomans had predicted a time of 9.66 UT February 1986 while Brady's calculations of 9.39 UT February 1986 was an even closer result. A prediction of 5.37 UT February 1986, calculated by a computer several decades earlier but using Newtonian theory only, seems to confirm that non-gravitational forces, at present amounting to three to four days per revolution, are still at work and affecting the comet by the amount Cowell and Crommelin themselves suspected in 1909.

During 1984-5 the comet gradually brightened until it came within range of smaller telescopes. Any naked-eye sightings could not be expected before December 1985, at the earliest, but long before this it began to receive the widest publicity from the popular media and with it much of the razzmatazz reminiscent of that afforded the ill-fated Kohoutek comet a decade earlier which from the public's point of view turned out to be a damp squib.

Even the *Wall Street Journal*, a publication not previously known for its comet reportage, now provided regular dispatches about the various business enterprises marshalling their efforts to exploit fully the heaven-sent opportunity to flood the consumer markets with anything that might possibly be labelled and packaged with a comet motif. Souvenirs on sale ranged from expensive warm-up jackets (to be worn to view the comet) embossed with the appropriate logo . . . to cocktail glasses etched with quaint verses for toasting the comet on the celebratory night of its perihelion passage. Already on sale in New York by January 1985 were at least sixteen different brands of Halley T-shirts, and the numbers of these proliferated world-wide every month the comet drew closer.

Not to miss out on their share of the comet bonanza, shipping companies and airlines feverishly advertised lavish excursions to the tropics and to the southern skies where it was predicted the comet would be much better placed for viewing.

On a less mundane plane, the modern-day gloom-and-doom pamphleteers, worthy successors to their forbears at the time of the Plague and Fire comets, were kept busy penning their dire threats of Armageddon.

In response to all these semi-hysterical manifestations of the human condition there were comet lovers, with fingers crossed, promising little, quietly awaiting the sight of one of nature's free spectacles and hoping that not too many would-be viewers are let down by the weather and driven to echoing the frustration of that anonymous poet in *Punch* circa 1910 . . .

To attempt to view the comet in the light-polluted streets of a city is courting disappointment from the start. To attempt to view it during bright moonlit nights, without knowing *exactly* where to look, is likewise inviting frustration – as was Sam Pepys's experience when he first tried to view the Plague comet back in 1664. The best time of all to see it should be in March or early April 1986 after the comet has passed its perihelion. It will then probably be seen as a fuzzy 2^m star adorned with a 30 to 40° tail. However, the unexpected *usually* happens with comets, and it may be brighter or fainter than this.

Whatever its brightness or impact on the public at this very favourable time, by May 1986 it will have faded again beyond naked-eye vision. Long after the comet itself has passed into oblivion, we may perhaps anticipate one likely aftermath of its presence in the skies in 1986. No doubt astute vintners, rubbing their hands, have already dusted off those fascinating, old wine catalogues and noted with satisfaction the glowing approbation their great-great-grandfathers gave to the legendary vintage following the 1811 comet.

Whether the '86 will deserve such accolades, only time will tell.

Appendices

APPENDIX 1: MISSIONS PLANNED TO HALLEY'S COMET

Giotto Mission The European Space Agency's (ESA) mission to Halley's comet is appropriately named *Giotto*, after the Florentine painter Giotto de Bondone, whose realistic depiction of a comet, possibly Halley's in 1301, adorns the fresco he painted in the Scovegni Chapel in Padua.

The planned launch date for this mission is scheduled for July 1985 from Kourou in French Guiana. It will use an Ariane vehicle in tandem with a second project, and the first step is to send it into a high elliptical orbit from where the comet-probe's onboard engine can be fired to inject it into a Halley-transfer orbit. After a cruise lasting seven months, the probe should reach the comet on 13 March 1986, a little over one month after perihelion. At this time the comet is 0.98 AU distant from the Sun and 1 AU distant from the Earth. If all goes well, it will pass within 500 km of the comet, during which time it will be moving at 68 km per second. Because there is a real possibility of the probe being 'sandblasted' by particles of dust ejected from the comet and a consequent risk of total destruction, any information gleaned by the probe's battery of ten instruments is to be relayed to Earth immediately.

Planet A Mission The Tokyo Institute of Space and Astronomical Science (ISAS) plan to send a probe, named *Planet A*, to fly past Halley's comet on 8 March 1986, or about five days before the ESA Giotto mission. A test-vehicle, named MS-T5 was successfully launched in January 1985 prior to the actual mission launch to check its capability in manoeuvring and positioning. Actual mission launch is scheduled for 14 August 1985 from the Kagoshima Space Centre in Southern Japan. A booster-motor in the back of the probe will give it extra kick to position it in a comet-intercept trajectory. Unlike other probes which make use of a parking orbit round the Earth, the Japanese one is direct injection. While this method favours fuel conservation, once set on course it cannot later be corrected. As a consequence its anticipated closest encounter with the comet may be no nearer than some tens of thousands of kilometres from the comet's nucleus.

Vega 1 and 2   The Halley's comet mission planned by the Soviet Union is one coupled with a mission to Venus. Two identical space vehicles, *Vega 1* and *2*, were launched to Venus in the middle of December 1984. After carrying Venus landing-probes, which arrive mid-June 1985, both vehicles then make use of the planet's gravity field to redirect them and set them on intercept courses with the comet. If the manoeuvres are successful, the first vehicle will encounter Halley's comet on 8 March 1986 and the second about a week later. The second back-up probe allows the Soviet mission planners alternative encounter options. While either probe can be targeted with a claimed precision of about 100 km, the first will probably be manoeuvred for a safe 10,000 km stand-off. If the first probe is successful, the second may then be risked for a very close-encounter 'sandblasting' to obtain a bird's-eye view of the inner coma regions and the long elusive nucleus.

Additional Notes   The main Japanese probe, Planet A, is scheduled to pass within 200,000km, and its prime function will be to obtain ultra-violet pictures of the nucleus from the sunward side of the comet.

Each Soviet Vega probe is equipped with various combinations of instruments, but the primary ones are two cameras (per probe) mounted on platforms which can swivel to follow the comet as it sweeps by. One camera in each combination has a wider angle than the other to take in an overall view of the coma regions and (hopefully) spot the precise location of the nucleus. The second camera has a narrower field and is to be targeted directly at the nuclear regions to provide a resolution of detail larger than 200m. By the use of different filters the images obtained of the comet by both cameras can later be combined to provide full colour pictures of the comet's interior for transmission back to Earth.

Compared with the Soviet and Japanese probes, ESA's Giotto probe offers the most dramatic encounter. Because it is targeted to fly by the comet to within 500km, it has already been billed as a kamikaze mission. It is estimated the probe will be within the comet's tenuous atmosphere for as long as four hours. During that time it could hit one or more dust particles in the coma, and because the comet and probe will be travelling in opposite directions, their encounter velocity will be high. In concrete terms, one authority suggests that if a 0.1 gram particle hits the side of the probe, this will have the same kinetic energy as a 600kg car driven at 100km per hour.

To reduce the danger to Giotto's instrumentation the probe is equipped with a dust shield in the form of a two-layered bumper. The first bumper is constructed of aluminium 1mm thick, and it is supposed that small particles will be absorbed by this. However, a larger particle will go straight through it and vaporize in the process. As a result the second layer made of Kevlar and foam will then hopefully absorb the impact without causing the path of the probe to deviate and thus affect communications with Earth.

As Giotto enters the comet's atmosphere, it will have its dust shield at the bow end and the sensitive communication antenna pointing earthwards at the stern. The crux of the whole mission is Giotto's communication system, for if it fails to mainain its correct orientation, no signals will reach the Earth. The transmission beam is ultra-sensitive to direction. A deviation by as little as one degree will cause loss of contact. Timing for the mission is hypercritical. Travelling at 68/9km/s at its scheduled rendezvous distance of 500km, Giotto will be alongside the comet for only 14 seconds. Its last orbital manoeuvre is planned to occur two days before its scheduled 13 March 1986 intercept. If the Soviet Vega mission controllers agree to co-operate and pass on information received back from the first of the Vega probes (which reaches the comet before Giotto), this will prove vital for Giotto's own controllers, allowing them to make last minute adjustments in trajectory.

If all goes according to plan, we may anticipate that some time after early March 1986 we can all sit back in front of our own TV screens to be treated to some of the most dramatic pictures ever to reach us from space.

APPENDIX 2: COMET NOMENCLATURE – HOW COMETS ARE NAMED AND RECORDED

The International HQ for monitoring comets is the (IAU) Central Bureau for Astronomical Telegrams at Cambridge, Mass, USA. This organization publishes telegrams announcing new discoveries and recoveries and periodically issues *Circulars* with update information.

Every year brings under observation a score or more of comets. Some of these are known periodic comets returning; others are new ones never seen before. In order to keep track of all these comings and goings, a system has been evolved whereby each comet is separately tagged, using a precise nomenclature, from the time of its discovery or, if a returning comet, its recovery.

In the first instance an alphabetical system is applied, and in this way the first comet sighted in 1981 was provisionally labelled 1981a, the second comet 1981b, etc.

This alphabetical system is independent of the discoverer's name-tag – only applied if the comet is a new one. This provisional system allows for the elimination of discoveries which are announced but subsequently not seen again and therefore remain unconfirmed objects. A year or so later, when the orbits of new or returning comets have been thoroughly investigated, each is allocated a permanent Roman numeral: comet 1981 I, comet 1981 II, etc. in order of its perihelion passage. These then become definitive designations which stand for all time in the comet catalogues where entries are arranged in chronological order of perihelion. Thus, for example, comet 1981a was finally designated comet 1981 XVI since, although it was the first to be sighted in 1981, it later proved to be the sixteenth in order of its perihelion passage that year; while 1981b proved to be the eleventh and so was finally listed as comet XI. When Halley's comet was resighted in 1983, it was provisionally tagged 1983i, but its final designation for its 1986 apparition will not be known for a year or so after its predicted perihelion passage in February 1986.

Apart from the provisional Arabic letter and definitive Roman numeral, a comet also carries the name of its discoverer or discoverers. This sometimes leads to complications if a number of people independently discover the same comet as often happens when it is a bright one (*see also note 2, chapter 9*). To overcome this thorny problem it has been internationally agreed that no more than three names shall be attached to any one comet. Occasionally, but very rarely, if the comet is very bright and is noticed by many people almost simultaneously, it will receive no personal name and will subsequently be listed in the catalogues under Daylight Comet, Brilliant Comet or Great Comet, or sometimes it will carry a geographical designation, for example: Southern Comet 1947 XII (1947n); or Parisian Comet 1759 III. A comet may also have a name referring to a man-made artifact. For example, when comet 1983d was independently discovered visually by the Japanese astronomer C. Araki, the British veteran comet hunter G.E.D. Alcock and then also detected automatically by the orbiting Infrared Astronomical Satellite (IRAS), it was subsequently named comet IRAS-Araki-Alcock.

Periodic comets can be recognized in catalogue nomenclature and in literature by the prefix P; thus comet 1910 II is fully listed as: P/Halley 1910 II (1909c). Note that although Halley's was the third comet resighted in 1909, it did not come to perihelion until 1910.

Usually when a periodic comet is reobserved, it does not require any new or additional names. However, there are exceptions to this rule. For example, when comet P/Perrine was missed for six of its scheduled returns and then rediscovered quite by accident by the Czech comet hunter Anton Mrkos in 1955, it was decided to rename it P/Perrine-Mrkos.

A comet may also bear a name other than its discoverer's, and Halley's comet provides the most famous example. A more recent example was the renaming of a comet that once went under the awkward title (and broke the three-name rule) of P/Pons-Coggia-Winnecke-Forbes. In place of this tongue-twisting, compound name it was decided to redesignate it

P/Crommelin in honour of the British computer A.C.D. Crommelin of Halley's comet prediction fame in 1909-10, who also investigated the orbit of this other comet with a similar thoroughness.

APPENDIX 3: THE ORBIT OF A COMET

In order to determine the path of a comet round the Sun, six elements are required to be known:

1 The perihelion distance of the comet (or distance from the Sun at its closest approach).
2 Its heliocentric longitude (a position in relation to the Sun usually termed the argument of perihelion, *see Fig. 14*).
3 The position of the nodes (or where the path of the comet crosses the plane of the ecliptic).
4 The inclination of the comet's orbit to the plane of the ecliptic.
5 The exact time of perihelion passage.
6 The period of the comet's revolution.

To calculate an orbit a computer requires a minimum of three observations separated by time intervals (preferably several days between each). To find the six orbital elements, six independent quantities (two in each observation) must be obtained either by direct visual observations or, more accurately, by measurements of the comet's image recorded on photographic plates. These are coordinate measurements of Right Ascension (RA) and Declination (Dec) – analogous to terrestrial longitude and latitude – obtained by angular offsets to adjacent field stars

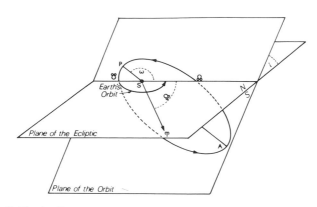

Fig. 14   Orbit of a Comet

S   = *Sun.*
♈   = First point of Aries.
P   = Perihelion (nearest point of the orbit to the Sun).
A   = Aphelion (farthest point of the orbit from the Sun).
ω   = Argument of perihelion (the angle) from the ascending node to the perihelion measured in the plane of the ecliptic.
☊   = Ascending node (point where the orbit intersects the plane of the ecliptic, the comet moving northwards [N]).
☋   = Descending node (point were the orbit intersects the plane of the ecliptic, the comet moving southwards [S]).
i   = Inclination of the orbit to the ecliptic plane.

whose positions are recorded in various catalogues and known to a high degree of accuracy and then corrected for all known variable factors.

Unlike the major planets, many comets move in paths that are inclined to the ecliptic at steep angles. When their inclinations exceed 90°, comets are said to possess retrograde orbits round the Sun (e.g. Halley's comet which is inclined at 162.2°). These retrograde comets revolve in a clockwise direction, i.e. the opposite (reverse) motion to that of the planets.

The distinction between short- and long-period comets is hazy, but one may say any comet with a period of *less* than 150-200 years is one of short period. Some long-period comets which have highly elongated elliptical paths, such as the Sungrazers, can never be given accurate orbital periods owing to the close similarity of their ellipses to a true parabola; thus their orbital periods round the Sun may range between anything from 1,000 to 100,000 years or more.

APPENDIX 4: MAGNITUDE, OR BRIGHTNESS, OF A COMET

As with other celestial objects the apparent brightness of a comet is expressed in terms of its stellar magnitude. The system is based on an idea first adopted by the Greek astronomer Hipparchus (in the 2nd century BC) who divided all the visible stars into six grades of brightness. The very brightest he called 1st magnitude stars, the next 2nd magnitude and so on down to the 6th – which is approximately the faintest star that can be seen on a clear moonless night with the unassisted eye.

In more modern times Hipparchus's system was modified to upgrade the very brightest stars to zero (0) and minus (–) magnitudes. Thus Sirius, the brightest visible star, is magnitude (mag) – 1.4 while the planet Venus at her brightest is mag – 4.4. On the same (logarithmic) scale the Moon shines at mag – 12.7 and the Sun at mag – 26.7.

Because a comet is usually seen as a diffuse cloud-like source (as opposed to the point-source star), it is customary to express its magnitude in terms of the out-of-focus (extrafocal) image of a comparison star. Thus a (bright) comet estimated at mag 1 is in effect the equivalent brightness of a 1st magnitude star put slightly out of focus to form a disk of light approximating in size to that of the (in-focus) comet. With a faint photographic comet the magnitude may often refer to the nuclear region only since no surrounding envelope may be visible.

Biographical Note

Unlike his contemporary and friend Isaac Newton, original sources for Edmond Halley's life are very limited and there are lacunas spanning several years at a time. An article in *Biographia Britannia* (1757) is thought to have been written by Thomas Birch or John Machin from material prepared by Halley's son-in-law Henry Price, who was married to Catherine Halley (1688?-1765).

Another manuscript about Halley was found in the Bodleian Library at Oxford. It was transcribed by Stephen Peter Rigaud and possibly supplied the source of information for the 'Eloge de M Halley' by Dortous de Mairan, published in *Memoirs de l'Academie Royale des Sciences (Histoire)*, Paris 1742. This later appeared under the name of Bernard Fontenelle (in English) in the *Gentleman's Magazine* Vol XVII, 1747.

In the nineteenth century a bundle of manuscripts relating to Halley's life contained in material left by John Machin, onetime Secretary to the Royal Society, was lodged in the Library of the Royal Astronomical Society in London but this subsequently disappeared. Likewise, little is known about Halley's personal library, although it is believed these volumes were amalgamated into the Library of the Royal Observatory at Greenwich.

The prime (but unfortunately incomplete) modern source for Halleiana is contained in E.F. MacPike, *Correspondence and Papers of Edmond Halley* (Oxford 1932; London 1937), and this, with its extensive list of references, provides the basis for all modern scholarship. Extremely useful secondary sources which contain assessments of Halley's various scientific achievements are Angus Armitage, *Edmond Halley*, London 1966; and Colin Ronan, *Edmond Halley: Genius in Eclipse*, London 1969. An excellent account of Halley's voyages, containing primary references not cited elsewhere, is in *The Three Voyages of Edmond Halley in Paramore 1698-1701* 2 Vols, edited by Norman J.W. Thrower and published by the Hakluyt Society (2nd Series 156-7) London 1981.

Among the numerous biographies of Newton two of the more readily accessible to general readers are Richard S. Westfall's monumental study *Never at Rest*, Cambridge 1980; and Frank E. Manuel, *A Portrait of Isaac Newton*, London 1980.

Other Select Sources and References

Anglo-Saxon Chronicles (1066)

Armitage, Angus, *John Kepler*, London 1966

Baily, Francis, *John Flamsteed*, London 1835

Bainbridge, John, *An Astronomical Description of the late Comet*, 1619

Bayle, Pierre, *Lettre sur la Comète*, 1682
   Pensées diverses sur la Comète, 1683

Berkeley, George, *The Analyst* (an attack on the infidel mathematician Edmond Halley), London 1734

Brady, Joseph, *Journal of the British Astronomical Association*, Vol 92

Calder, Nigel, *The Comet is Coming!*, London 1980

Central Bureau for Astronomical Telegrams, Cambridge, Mass, USA (Director Dr Brian Marsden)

Chambers, George F., *The Story of the Comets*, Oxford 1909, 1910

Clairaut, Alexis-Claude, *Théorie des Comètes*, Paris 1760

Comets, Asteroids, Meteorites: interrelations, evolution and origins, IAU Colloquium No 39, 1976, edited by Delsemme, A.H., Toledo 1977

Cowell, P.H. and Crommelin, A.C.D., *Essay on the Return of Halley's Comet*, Leipzig 1910

Dick, Oliver Lawson, *Aubrey's Brief Lives*, London 1960

Evelyn, John, *Evelyn's Diary*, Oxford 1955

Gadbury, John, *De Cometis*, London 1665
   London's Deliverance Predicted, London 1715

Guillemin, Amédée, *The World of Comets*, London 1877

Hearne, Thomas, *Remarks and Collections*, IV, Oxford 1884-1921

Hevelius, Johannes, *Cometographia*, Danzig 1668
    Annus Climactericus, Danzig 1685

Hind, J. Russell, *On the Expected Return of the Great Comet of 1264 and 1556*, London 1848
    Monthly Notices of the Royal Astronomical Society, 1850
    The Comets, London 1852

History of Science, Vol 3, Cambridge 1964

Hooke, Robert, *The Diary of, 1672-1680*, London 1968

Hoyle, F. and Wickramasinghe, N.C., *Lifecloud*, London 1978
    Diseases from Space, London 1979
    Evolution from Space London 1981
    Space Travellers – the Bringers of Life, Cardiff 1981

Hoyle, F., *The Intelligent Universe*, London 1983

Icarus, Vol 23, Number 4

Kepler, Johannes, *De cometis*, 1619

Kiang, T., *Observatory*, Vols 91, 93

Koestler, Arthur, *The Sleepwalkers*, London 1959

Kuiper, G.P. and Roemer, E., *Comets: Scientific Data and Missions*, Proceedings of the Tuscon Comet Conference, Tuscon 1972

Lalande, J.J., *Bibliographie Astronomique*, Paris 1803 (reprinted 1970)

Lancaster Brown, P., *Journal of the British Astronomical Association*, Vols 75, 76
    Comets, Meteorites & Men, London 1973, New York 1974
    Megaliths, Myths & Men – an introduction to astro-archaeology, Poole, New York 1976
    Megaliths & Masterminds, London, New York 1979

Lilly, William, *History of his Life and Times*, London 1715

Lindsay, Jack, *Origins of Astrology*, London 1971

Lubienieczki, Stanislas, *Theatrum Cometicum*, Amsterdam 1667 and 1668

Lynn, W.T., *The Observatory*, Vol 14, 347-8

Lyttleton, R.A., *The Comets and their Origins*, 1953

MacPike, E.F., *Hevelius, Flamsteed and Halley*, London 1937

Marsden, Brian, *Astronomical Journal*, 72, No 9, 1967
    Science, Vol 155, pp 1207-1213, 1967

Maupertuis, P.L. Moreau de, *Lettre sur La Comète*, Paris 1742

Milne, David, *Essay on Comets*, Edinburgh and London 1828

NASA, *The Study of Comets:* A conference held at Goddard Space Flight Center Greenbelt, Maryland 28 October – 1 November 1974,

Washington 1976

Nature, Vol 300, 239, 1982

Needham, Joseph, *Science and Civilization in China*, Vol 3, Cambridge 1959

Newton, Sir Isaac, *The Mathematical Principles of Natural Philosophy*, translated by Motte, Andrew, London 1729

A Dissertation on Comets, London c. 1750

Pepys, Samuel, *The Diary of Samuel Pepys,* (edited by Latham, Robert and Matthews, William), London 1983

Plummer, H.C., *Nature*, Vol 150, 249

Porter, J.G., *Comets and Meteor Streams*, London 1952

Proctor, Richard A., *St Paul's Magazine*, September 1871

Rawlinson, George, *History of Herodotus*, London 1880

Richter, N.B., *The Nature of Comets*, London 1963

Secretan, the Rev. C.F., *Memoirs of the Life and Times of the pious Robert Nelson*, 1860

Seneca, *Physical Science in the Time of Nero (Quaestiones Naturales)*, translated by Clarke, John, London 1910

Sky and Telescope, Vol 64, 551, 1982

Tacke, Johann, *Coeli Anomalon, id est, De Cometis,* 1653

Turner, H. H., *Halley's Comet*, Oxford 1908

Vsekhsvyatskii, S.K., *Physical Characteristics of Comets,* Jerusalem 1964 (although not always accurate, a prime source-book for past comet apparitions)

Whiston, William, *The Cause of the Deluge Demonstrated,* London 1714

Memoirs of the Life and Writings of Mr William Whiston, London 1749

Yeomans, Donald K., *The Comet Halley Handbook*, Washington 1982

See also text, *passim.*

Table 1: Parabolic Elements of 24 Comets (after Halley)

Date of Perihelion Passage	Ascending Node	Inclination	Motion	Perihelion Longitude	Perihelion Distance
1337 June 2 6 25	84°21' 0"	32°11' 0"	R	37°59' 0"	0.40666
1472 Feb. 28 22 23	281 46 20	5 20 0	R	45 33 30	0.54273
1531 Aug. 24 21 18	49 25 0	17 56 0	R	301 39 0	0.56700*
1532 Oct. 19 22 12	80 27 0	32 36 0	D	111 7 0	0.50910
1556 April 21 20 3	175 42 0	32 6 30	D	278 50 0	0.46390
1577 Oct. 26 18 45	25 52 0	74 32 45	R	129 22 0	0.18342
1580 Nov. 28 15 0	18 57 20	64 40 0	D	109 5 50	0.59628
1585 Sept. 27 19 20	37 42 20	6 4 0	D	8 51 0	1.09358
1590 Jan. 29 3 45	165 30 40	29 40 40	R	216 54 30	0.57661
1596 July 31 19 55	312 12 30	55 12 0	R	228 16 0	0.51293
1607 Oct. 16 3 50	50 21 0	17 2 0	R	302 16 0	0.58680*
1618 Oct. 29 12 23	76 1 0	37 34 0	D	2 14 0	0.37975
1652 Nov. 2 15 40	88 10 0	79 28 0	D	28 18 40	0.84750
1661 Jan. 16 23 41	82 30 30	32 35 50	D	115 58 40	0.44851
1664 Nov. 24 11 52	81 14 0	21 18 30	R	130 41 25	1.02575
1665 April 14 5 15	228 2 0	76 5 0	R	71 54 30	0.10649
1672 Feb. 20 8 37	297 30 30	83 22 10	D	46 59 30	0.69739
1677 April 26 0 37	236 49 10	79 3 15	R	137 37 5	0.28059
1680 Dec. 8 0 6	272 2 0	60 56 0	D	262 39 30	0.00612
1682 Sept. 4 7 39	51 16 30	17 56 0	R	302 52 45	0.58328*
1683 July 3 2 50	173 23 0	83 11 0	R	85 29 30	0.56020
1684 May 29 10 16	268 15 0	65 48 40	D	238 52 0	0.96015
1686 Sept. 6 14 33	350 34 40	31 21 40	D	77 0 30	0.32500
1698 Oct. 8 16 57	267 44 15	11 46 0	R	270 51 15	0.69129

*Halley's Comet

Table 2: Returns to Perihelion of Halley's Comet

240 (BC) May 15?	912 (AD) July 19
163 (BC) May 20?	989 (AD) Sept. 2 (Burckhardt)
87 (BC) Aug. 15	1066 (AD) Mar. 25 (Hind)
12 (BC) Oct. 8 (Hind)	1145 (AD) April 19 (Hind)
66 (AD) Jan. 26 (Hind)	1222 (AD) Sept. 10
141 (AD) Mar. 25 (Hind)	1301 (AD) Oct. 23 (Hind)
218 (AD) April 6 (Hind)	1378 (AD) Nov. 8 (Laugier)
295 (AD) April 7 (Hind)	1456 (AD) June 2 (Halley, Pingré)
374 (AD) Feb. 13 (Hind)	1531 (AD) Aug. 25 (Halley)
451 (AD) July 3 (Laugier)	1607 (AD) Oct. 26 (Halley)
530 (AD) Nov. 15 (Hind)	1682 (AD) Sept. 14 (Halley)
607 (AD) Mar. 26	1759 (AD) Mar. 12 (Halley)
684 (AD) Nov. 26 (Hind)	1835 (AD) Nov. 15
760 (AD) June 10 (Laugier)	1910 (AD) April 19
837 (AD) Feb. 25 (Hind)	1986 (AD) Feb. 9

Index